Lampong-râja 135[...]
  Angkor in 1352 an[...]
  throne. Lampong-r[...]
  regained his kingdom[...]

Sûryavamsa Râjâdhirâja, brother of Lampong-râja,
  1357 – c.1377

Paramarâma, a son of Lampong-râja c.1377 – c.1380

Dhammâsokarâjâdhirâja, brother of Paramarâma (known
  in Chinese records as Chao Ponhea Kambuja) c.1380 – ?

Râmeśvara of Siam occcupied Angkor in 1393 and
  placed a son of his on the throne but he is soon
  assassinated.

Samdach Chao Ponhea (presumably = Dhammâsokarâjâdhirâja) continues to rule until 1405, when his death is
  announced in Chinese sources.

Chao Ponhea Yat, seemingly known in Chinese records
  as Chao P'ing Ya. He later took the glorious name of
  Sûryavarman and he may also have received the
  posthumous name of Nippeanbât = *Nirvânapada*)
  1405 – ? During his reign the decision was made in
  1431 to move to Phnom Penh.

[1] This and the following dates are based upon the careful
reconstruction of Georges Coedès and have often been repeated
uncritically. For the most recent critical studies see Michael
Vickery, *Society, Economics and Politics in pre-Angkor
Cambodia*, pp.394-404, and also the article by Karl-Heinz
Golzio 'Consider-ations on the chronology and history of 9th
century Cambodia' in *Siksâcakr, Journal of the Khmer Cultural Centre 2*, October 2000, Siem Reap, Cambodia, pp.21-5.
Vickery places the Jayavarman's arrival in Cambodia around
770. One may assume he was about 20 at the time. If he died
as late as 850 he would be aged about 100. The year 834/5 is
a justifiable and certainly more plausible date. Golzio raises the
problem of two kings, Rudravarman and Pritthvîndravarman,
named by Yaśovarman as his predecessors in Prâsâd Preah Ko
(Ruluos), suggesting that they might have to be inserted as
reigning monarchs after Jayavarman III. However, they might
equally well have been given royal rank posthumously. Please
note that the date of 850 for Jayavarman's death remains
unchanged in my main text on p. 27.

[2] These records are supposed to begin from the year 1346. They
were prepared by a minister appointed to the task by royal
command in the first half of the 19th century in order to replace
those destroyed by earlier wars. They depend partly on the
Annals of Ayuthaya but are also a concoction of hearsay and
legend. As will be noted here some of these kings are also
mentioned in Chinese records but the names are seldom firmly
identifiable.

[3] The details of these last reigns is compiled mainly from G.Coedès,
Indianized States, pp.236-7. One may also refer usefully to
L.P.Briggs, *The Ancient Khmer Empire*, pp. 251-7. I have
tried to produce some coherence in the accounts, but my list
inevitably remains provisional.

ORCHID
GUIDES

KHMER CIVILIZATION
AND ANGKOR

DAVID SNELLGROVE

Orchid Press
Bangkok 2001 ❖ 2544 Buddhist Era

David L. Snellgrove
KHMER CIVILIZATION AND ANGKOR

First published 2001

Published by
Orchid Press
P. O. Box 19, Yuttitham Post Office
Bangkok 10907, Thailand

This book is printed on acid-free long-life paper
which meets the specifications of ISO 9706 / 1994.

ISBN 974-8304-95-7

CONTENTS

PREFACE

This book is intended for visitors to Cambodia and indeed for anyone who is interested in a brief account of the history and culture of this once great empire. A more voluminous account with a much more detailed bibliography may be found in the earlier work of Lawrence Palmer Briggs, *The Ancient Khmer Empire*, published in *Transactions of the American Philosophical Society*, new series, volume 41, Philadelphia 1951, reprinted in 1962 and 1974. I note that it has recently been reprinted as a new edition in Bangkok. This shorter work of mine consists of extracts from Chapters IX, XI and XII of a my much larger book, entitled *Asian Commitment, Travels and Studies in the Indian Sub-Continent and South-East Asia* (Orchid Press, Bangkok 2000).

I have lived off and on in Cambodia since 1995 and have witnessed the change from the period of "storm and stress", which followed the intervention by the United Nations in the early nineties to the relative stability of the country, achieved since the 1998 elections. Earlier it was unsafe to travel anywhere beyond the confines of Phnom Penh and Siem Reap (Angkor). Now with proper precautions, the primary need being staunch Khmer companionship, one can travel anywhere throughout the whole country.

My thanks are due to the Ministry of Foreign Affairs for permission to reside in Cambodia and to the École française de l'Extrême Orient which has harboured my endeavours under its well spread wings.[1] Personally I owe much to Monsieur Olivier de Bernon of the EFEO, who has constantly come to my assistance in practical affairs as well as in matters of literary research. I add that he is responsible for the finding and preservation of what now remains of Khmer monastic library collections (viz. Fonds pour l'édition des manuscrits de Camboge). It is estimated that at least 95 per cent of Cambodia's traditional literary heritage that existed before 1970 has been destroyed during the turbulent and terrible years of slaughter and destruction that followed.

Acknowledgements are also due to Pheung Vutthy and his brother Taing Joy, who like so many others lost all the rest of their family during the peremptory executions of the Pol Pot régime, and who since my first arrival in Cambodia have done much to integrate me into Khmer family-life. Vutthy has been my constant companion on all my travels in the country.

David Snellgrove
Siem Reap, June 1999

INTRODUCTION

This booklet is not arranged as a guide to the temples of Angkor, but is rather intended to show that this once great capital city was the centre of a Khmer empire which included most of Indo-China. It is thus a short history of of the Khmers with special reference to their archaeological sites throughout Indo-China. At the same time interest in Angkor predominates. Its proper name was Yaśodharapura, the "Glorious Citadel", having been founded by King Yaśovarman about the year 900. Angkor, deriving from Sanskrit *nagara*, means simply the "City", thus defining it as the one city that counted above all others.[2] The Khmers are known as a distinct race of people from the 6th century onwards and in this book their history is traced from their early beginnings as a group of petty kingdoms through the first attempts to establish a unified kingdom in the 7th century, known as Îsânapura (after its founder Îsânavarman). Later in the early 9th century another capital city was established at Hariharâlaya, leading directly to the foundation of Angkor several decades later. From then onwards

1 *The west front of Angkor Vat on the occasion of the opening of the Râmâyana Festival at the end of December 1995.*

the Khmers continued to extend their authority to the north and the west, establishing subsidiary citadels, where governors, nominally subject to Angkor, were installed. Temple-fortresses was built in all such places and many of these remain preserved throughout present-day Thailand. The Thais were comparatively late arrivals on the scene pressing down from the north and impinging upon the Khmer empire just when it had reached its greatest extent in the 13th century. From then on more and more territory was gradu-

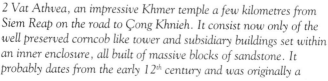
2 Vat Athvea, an impressive Khmer temple a few kilometres from Siem Reap on the road to Çong Khnieh. It consist now only of the well preserved corncob like tower and subsidiary buildings set within an inner enclosure, all built of massive blocks of sandstone. It probably dates from the early 12th century and was originally a

ally ceded to the Thais, as well also to the Vietnamese, until Cambodia was reduced to an even smaller size than now indicated by its present international boundaries.

For anyone interested in the history and culture of the Khmers, a visit to Angkor is really only the starting-point. Their temple fortresses, often in a badly ruined condition, are to be found throughout Cambodia, throughout Thailand, and also reaching into southern Laos as well as Vietnamese territory adjacent to the present southern Cambo-

ix

Brahmanic foundation. Surviving inscriptions from the 16th to 17th century prove that this shrine was then adapted to the use of a Theravâdin Buddhist community (as were Angkor Vat and other important shrines in Angkor itself) and it still forms the centre of just such a community. (See Aymonier, Le Camboge, II, p.398 f.)

dian frontier. The French who extended their control over Cambodia from 1863 have a done a great deal to list and preserve this enormous cultural heritage, and one might refer as examples to the great compendium of Étienne Aymonier, *Le Camboge*, published in Paris in three volumes from 1900-1904, or that of Lunet de Lajonquière, *Inventaire descriptif des monuments du Cambodge*, 3 vols, Paris 1902-11, or again that of H. Parmentier, *L'art Khmer primitif*, published in two volumes in Paris in 1927. It will be noted that most of the works quoted in my bibliography are inevitably in French. It is unfashionable nowadays to praise any aspects of imperial rule in former colonies and protec-

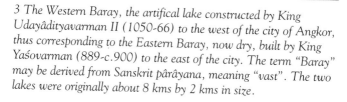

3 *The Western Baray, the artifical lake constructed by King Udayâdityavarman II (1050-66) to the west of the city of Angkor, thus corresponding to the Eastern Baray, now dry, built by King Yaśovarman (889-c.900) to the east of the city. The term "Baray" may be derived from Sanskrit pârâyana, meaning "vast". The two lakes were originally about 8 kms by 2 kms in size.*

torates, but it can be fairly stated that the French, apart from their sustained archaeological research-work, have also saved Cambodia from becoming a mere dependency of Thailand. Thanks to French pressure the provinces of Battembang sand Siem Reap (including therefore Angkor) which had been annexed by the Thais, were restored to

Cambodia in 1907, and with the formal granting of independence in 1953 Cambodia was firmly established as a sovereign country. However its history since then has not been a happy one.[3]

Norodom Sihanouk (born 1922), who came to the throne in 1941 under French (Vichy) suzerainty, continued to rule under the restored French colonial administration with the ending of World War II and the departure of the Japanese occupiers (1945 onwards). In 1953 he succeeded in gaining independence from the French by an extraordinary process of bluff and persuasion at a time when they were bitterly involved in their war with the Viet-Minh. However, just as in British India and in the Dutch East Indies (now Indonesia), there already existed in Indo-China vociferous groups who envisaged national independence as also bringing with it a "Utopian" form of government. The intellectual leaders of such groups were usually students who had been able to study in Britain, Holland or France. Here they were liable to come into close contact with Communist groups, with the result that the parties demanding independence in their home countries (especially Indo-China and the Dutch East Indies) were mainly Communist with the usual revolutionary ideas of transforming society from the top down. King Sihanouk´s main problems were to suppress any groups that threatened his autocratic form of rule and to keep the country neutral with regard to the war raging in Vietnam, to which far greater ferocity was added by the later massive American involvement. In neither of these problems was he eventually successful. Forced to come to terms with the North Vietnamese, he made a secret agreement, allowing them to station troops in Cambodia and also to import arms and supplies across Cambodian territory. Meanwhile Khmer Communist groups remained encamped near the border under Vietnamese protection. With the growing victory of the North Vietnamese and the withdrawal of American troops in 1973, the Communist-armed infiltration into Cambodia began.

Meanwhile Sihanouk was deposed in 1970 by his own National Assembly and the leaders of the republic attempted vainly to drive the Vietnamese from the country, which gradually fell under occupied Communist control. In early 1973 the USA began a series of massive bombing raids on Cambodia in order to stem this Communist advance. It may have delayed the eventual fall of Phnom Penh in 1975 but an appalling amount of destruction and loss of life was inflicted vainly on ordinary simple Cambodians (Khmers).

The leaders of the new administration established in the country were Saloth Sar (better known as Pol Pot) and Ieng Sary, both of whom had been students in Paris. They resolved to create in record time a "utopian" society in the name of the simple village folk. Michael Vickery in his *Cambodia 1975-82* draws attention to a long-standing antipathy existing between city-folk, especially in Phnom Penh, who were benefitting from the adjuncts of modern civilization, and the country-folk, who continued their centuries-old daily grind. Pol Pot and his followers exploited this division. Their "re-education programmes", largely consisting of hard work, may not have been always negative in the early stages in areas where the local supervisors were reasonable men. But by 1977 the system was already breaking down with mutual recriminations and the beginnings of wholesale killings. In the brief course of their three and a half years of rule they slaughtered close on a million of their fellow-countrymen, put an end to all normal social and religious life, while reducing most of the population to intense hardship (through forced labour) and in many areas starvation. As in the case of the Chinese "Great Leap Forward" of 1958-60, with its attempt to eliminate the differences between town and countryside, in the Cambodian case the town-dwellers were driven out to work on the land, while those of higher education and social position, as potentially unconvertible to the new doctrine, were rooted out and disposed of, especially from 1977 onwards. Buddhist monasteries, mosques and churches were destroyed in this later period, as well as schools and col-

xii

leges. Even ancient monuments were sometimes recklessly disfigured.

Leaders of the "Khmer Rouge" (the term coined by the French for Pol Pot and his followers) then turned their attentions upon members of their own following who were regarded in any way as unreliable. Determined that this should be an exemplary Khmer revolution, the leadership denied earlier affiliation with Vietnamese Communism and set about slaughtering Vietnamese as well. This provoked the Vietnamese invasion of early 1979, which drove Pol Pot and his followers into the Thai borderlands and resulted in a relatively mild form of Vietnamese suzerainty. The slaughtering came to an end and the right to private property was reinstated, enabling the survivors to return to their villages to reclaim their lands and thus reconstitute normal village life. Schools, monasteries and mosques began to be rebuilt, a long process which continues even today.

Internationally Vietnam was still treated as a pariah nation, especially by the USA, which now gave its support to the considerable Khmer Rouge remants in Thai border areas, treating them in effect as anti-Vietnamese and thus anti-Communist allies.[4] The only effective foreign relations of Vietnamese-occupied Cambodia were with Russia and its satellite neighbours in eastern Europe. Thus the subject Khmers, living in an enclosed Communist environment, had no political freedom and no contact with their other non-Communist neighbours. However the Vietnamese deserve some credit for starting the rehabilitation of the country after the totally destructive years of the Khmer Rouge. This work of reconstruction was carried forward by the UNO in the early 1990s, and still continues under local Khmer enterprise, while King Norodom Sihanouk is once again on his throne.

During the ten years of the Vietnamese occupation (1979-89) the Khmer Rouge continued to receive arms and equipment both from China and from the USA. This enabled them to infiltrate and reoccupy large areas of the country. Only gradually have they been persuaded by superior force or more often by generous terms of surrender to recognize the present government. So generous are these terms that they are sometimes left "legally" in control of the area which they already occupy, on the understanding that they support the political party instrumental in arranging their "surrender". As they continue to bear arms, such arrangements increase the risk of bitter political antagonisms in the country. Few foreigners have been affected in practice, but anyone who enters rashly into an uncontrolled area is under risk of stepping upon one of the myriad land mines which still litter the country or of being taken captive by some free-roving Khmer Rouge or other bandits who will expect a ransom for his release. Thus only gradually has it become possible to travel safely beyond the limits of the capital and of Siem Reap, a major tourist centre.

Over the last twenty years the archaeological heritage of the country has suffered more deliberate depredations than at any time since the French authorities interested themselves in the preservation of these amazing monuments. Heads are sawn off statues, carved images are cut out from the stone work, and whole stone-carved plaques are removed. These are transported into Thailand for sale to foreign "art-collectors" in the art-shops of Bangkok. Such operations require the skilful planning of military groups, whether Khmer Rouge or government troops, who happen to control a particular area.

These depredations have continued until very recently and only since September 1998 when a stable government was finally establised in Phnom Penh has their been any hope of saving what now remains of Cambodia's cultural heritage. By contrast Khmer temples in Thailand have been well cared for by the Fine Arts Department of the Thai Government, and visitors who have the time at their disposal might well extend their journey in order to visit at least the great temple-fortresses of Phimai, Phnom Rung and Muang Tam, all within reach of the Nakhon Ratchasima on the Khorat Plateau. An excellent guidebook is available, covering these and many other sites, by

Michael Freeman, *A Guide to Khmer Temples in Thailand and Laos*, River Books, Bangkok 1996. By contrast visits to other important sites in Cambodia itself are not so easily arranged. My personal experience suggests that it is now safe to travel almost anywhere in Cambodia, if one can accept the often harsh conditions of travel. One rightly hears much about the dangers of land-mines and sadly local people still suffer greatly from them. But no traveller need depart from a route which has already been traversed by so many local people and which is known to be safe. Thus when visiting such sites as Phnom Banon near Battambang, one readily obtains advice from anyone nearby which is the safe route to the summit. As a foreigner I am always accompanied by a Khmer companion and this is surely a minimum precaution.

xv

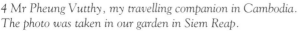

4 *Mr Pheung Vutthy, my travelling companion in Cambodia. The photo was taken in our garden in Siem Reap.*

That he has never visited the site before is a secondary consideration, and it would be very difficult indeed to find a local guide for sites other than Angkor itself. To give some idea of what may be involved in such travel I quote here an account of just such a journey made in February 2000, as sent to my publisher.

I have just returned from an adventurous excursion in order to find out if it is practicable to visit from the Cambodian side the temple-fortress of Preah Vihear (10th to 13th centuries, now a picturesque ruin) perched at 600 metres on a spur of the Dangrek Range which form the present Thai/Cambodian frontier. The Cambodians regained it from the Thais as the result of a court ruling at the Hague in 1962. I visited it last year from the Thai side, which is easy if you happen to be in that remote SE corner of Thailand. Ably supported by Vutthy I have just got back here on the 5th day of travel. On page 454 of my book Asian Commitment I have written that the approach to Preah Vihear is only practicable from the Thai side. This was surely re-peated from hearsay, and I suddenly began wondering whether this was really true. We could obtain no precise information in Siem Reap.

xvi

We knew only that we must set out towards Kampong Thom (namely in a SE direction) whence we could follow a road going north to Preah Vihear Province, where information would certainly be avail-able. The roads are all so bad in this part of Cambodia that there was no question of using our own light vehicle. We first hired the front seats in a small truck to Kampong Thom (150 kms from here - five hours of travel) and from there another going due north to a rather miserable place named Tbeng Meanchey on the map. This was 160 kms distant and another five hours along a track which became ever more difficult. This place is the capital of Preah Vihear Province, and is thus referred to by everyone locally as Preah Vihear, the name of the temple-fortress itself which is 140 kms still further north. It was night by the time we arrived at Tbeng Meanchey, which was quite as much unknown to Vutthy as myself. The driver dropped us off at the only available "guest house" where we were given two small grubby rooms, each with elementary toilet arrangements. We found one simple restaurant with an earthen floor, open to the street. The tables were filled with local people who sat watching a television, turned to its maximum sound-range. However a place was made for us and a good dish of noodles was soon prepared, while the owner sat nearby to ask who we might be and for what reason we had come. Thus at last we obtained some clear information about how to approach our final objective. Following his advice Vutthy soon found the next morn-ing another small truck to take us through the forest (no proper road) to an even more remote place named Chum Ksan. This was 70 kms distant and involved three hours of bumping travel. Having arrived in this sprawling village we had a midday meal at a wayside stall while deciding what our next move should be. As you may well imag-

ine foreigners are very rare in such remote places, so a small crown gathered around us while we ate. We now learned that we must take two motor-cycles for another 57 kms through the forest to the foot of the mountain, where we would find some soldiers in a hut who might be helpful. We easily found two youths with m/cs willing to carry us. As we swerved in the sand of the rough track out of Chum Ksan, I really thought: Is this my last foolish adventure? and I was tempted to return, admit defeat and spend the night in that wretched place. However we continued and courage returned. By 4 pm we reached the hut with three Khmer soldiers at the foot of our mountain, and one of them agreed to accompany us as guide and carry our gear. We could see Preah Vihear 600 metres above us. There was no one else around and nothing to eat or drink (except a small pool with muddy water), but we had brought our own drinking water, and some bananas and cold rice. The climb took two and a half hours to another small military post just below the final climb up to this old temple-fortress. Four Khmer monks have a temple-hut nearby. I was dead tired and wanted only to bathe (in a muddy pool) and sleep, while Vutthy had a meal of rice and stewed meat with the soldiers. The soldiers made room for Vutthy for the night, while the monks made room for me. One of them played with a radio until after midnight, and was sitting up playing with it again at 5 a.m. Local people sleep soundly through all such disturbances, but we westerners seem to be more sensitive creatures. We were up and about before dawn, thus completing the climb up to the first temple-gateway (gopura) just as the sun was rising. Thence one continues climbing up the massive stone causeway through a series of temple- gateways until one reaches the main shrine on the summit. It is badly ruined after its long occupation by the Khmer Rouge. No one else was around. The views are normally superb, but at that early hour mist still obscured much of the view of the Cambodian side. One could see the well-metalled road which makes the approach from the Thai side so easy, while on the Cambodian side one looked down from the sheer summit cliff to the vast extent of forest 600 metres below. There is no sign of human habitation, since the few small villages which we had passed are lost to view amongst the trees. At 7 am one or two Khmer guards arrived from the Thai side and soon afterwards the first Thai tourists. Especially welcome for us was a woman who opened a small stall to sell refreshments. She advised us that descending below the first temple-gateway on the Thai side, we would find some food-stalls amply provided with victuals. Thus fortified we made our back across to the Khmer side of the range, and having collected our belongings and remunerated the soldiers and the monks for their help, we made our way down the steep mountain-track. It was noon and very hot when we finally arrived at the bottom, where the two motor-cyclists had returned to pick us up, as agreed the evening before. Thus we made the long and dusty way back to Chum Ksan, pillion-riding and holding fast to our motor-cyclist champions, who make their way over ruts and between tree-roots or who kicked their way through stretches of deep sand.

5 *The first entrance-arch* (gopura) *at Preah Vihear on the crest of the Dangrek Range.*

We had to spend the night in Chum Ksan and soon found the only available guest-house with rooms more open and airy than those of the previous night. However mosquitos abounded. Nets hung over the beds and in any case we had brought with us an anti-mosquito spray. While I was washing in a kind of bath-house, my Cyma watch disappeared. (The gold one stays safely in a draw in Siem Reap.) It has great sentimental value as I bought it in Aden on the way by sea to India in 1953. I searched and Vutthy searched doubly amongst our limited belongings. It was useless to pursue further enquiries in such a place, especially as Vutthy suggested that it might have shaken *off my wrist on the 2-hour m/c ride. Certainly I got off my pillion feeling so sick that I was sure of nothing for the next hour or more. So I sadly reconciled myself to its loss.*

We passed the whole of the next morning covering the 70 kms back to Tbeng Meanchey, where we ordered the same dish of noodles in the same restaurant. The owner wanted to know details of our successful visit to the temple-fortress, as no one around had ever thought of going there. We had intended from here to make a detour to visit Koh Ker, an alternative Khmer capital city built by Jayavarman IV in the 10th century, but soon abandoned by his successors. This had been recently ransacked by government troops stationed there, but on this rare occasion the trucks carrying the dismantled stone pieces were fortunately apprehended and the stolen pieces deposited for safe keeping at the office of the Conservation d'Angkor in Siem Reap. However I was feeling too exhausted for this and in any case we had been advised that Koh Ker was still strewn with land-mines, although with local guidance a way could certainly be found between them. Thus wisdom prevailed and we spent the rest of the day covering the 150 kms back to Kampong Thom. Here at last there is a comfortable hotel with loud Koreake music and singing continuing until one in the morning, but we knew from previous experience that this can be avoided by taking a room on the top floor. As I opened one of the two small bags, there was the Cyma watch right on top like an unexpected gift from heaven. We have thought and though how it got there, but can find no solution. This "adventure" so far had taken four days. This was more than we had planned and so we did well to postpone the visit to Koh Ker to another occasion. On the 5th morning we easily found a truck to drive us back to Siem Reap.

Thus the statement that the only practicable way to reach Preah Vihear is from the Thai side certainly stands as it is, now proved to my personal satisfaction.

xix

Someone reading this, rather younger than myself, might think that there is nothing at all unusual about such a journey, and that if this is typical of travel in Cambodia, then all is really quite straightforward. One replies that it would probably be easy the second time. A main risk consists in not knowing in advance just what problems one may have to confront. Another risk consists in the possibility of a serious accident in so remote a place. For this same reason it may be difficult to find a responsible Khmer companion to accompany one on such a journey. He may quite rightly plead that if anything untoward happens to a foreigner in some remote part of the country, he himself will be held responsible for agreeing to accompany him on such a journey.

Nevertheless there are important sites which can be reached

with fair ease. Phnom Kulen can easily be reached from Siem Reap. However it is sad to relate that since this area has been so long in the hands of warring factions, practically nothing of archaeological interest remains. The ancient 7th century city of Îsânapura situated in the jungle at Sambor Prei Kuk can be reached from Kampong Thom either on motor-cyles or with a hired vehicle. However it may take about two hours to cover the 32 kms involved. The important temple-fortress of Bantay Chmar, some 60 kms north of Sisophon, can be reached by taking a truck from Siem Reap the 150 kms to Sisophon along the A6, and motor-cycles or a suitable vehicle from there. This will involve spending the night in Sisophon, but there are several hotels there. Ta Prohm and Phnom Chisor can be visited along the road from Phnom Penh to Kampot. Angkor Borei can be reached from Phnom Chisor – some 40 kms of rough gravel road.

The four temples mentioned in this booklet in the vicinity of Battambang can also be easily reached by the same means of transport. The difficulty of travel in many cases is caused by the very bad condition of the roads. When these are repaired as now promised, especially the A6 from Kampong Thom to Siem Reap, then on to Sisphon and the frontier with Thailand at Poipet, life will be very much easier. At present there is no great difficulty in travelling from Siem Reap to Bangkok by road, except for the stretch as far as Sisophon. From Aranyapathet, four kms the other side of the frontier, good air-conditioned buses will take one to Bangkok in a few hours, or conversely towards Nakhon Ratchasima, if one wants to visit some of the best of the Khmer temples to be seen in Thailand. However unless one speaks some Khmer or has a Khmer companion by one side it may not be easy to procure front seats in a truck on the Cambodian side. More hardy travellers readily mount the open part of the truck behind, enduring the heat and overwhelming clouds of dust. However all will become easy with the improvement of the roads and the introduction of regular bus-services. South of Kampong

6 Ploughing and the planting of rice, a regular sight when the monsoon rains arrive in June.

Thom to Phnom Penh and Kampong Cham the roads are already good. I note in passing that Bantay Prei Nokor is easily reached from Kampong Cham. The road from Phnom Penh to the frontier with Vietnam is also good, as well as the roads to Kampot and Kep by the sea and especially the road to Kampong Saom, which has a fine sea-coast with pleasant beaches. Cambodia has much to offer and gradually more and more possibilities will become available.

✳

As already explained above the Khmers have suffered much in recent years. Apart from the untold thousands or million and more who suffered torture and death at the hands of their own fellow-countrymen, the Khmer Rouge destroyed in four years the whole sub-structure of the country. Responsible bureaucracy, transport facilities, general education, medical facilities, religious life, archaeology, architecture, art and literature, all suffered the same fate.

✳

7 *The entrance to Bantay Ta Prohm (Kandal Province), some 30 kms south of Phnom Penh, Buddhist, 12ᵗʰ-13ᵗʰ century.*

8 *Four-armed Avalokiteśvara on the southern upper wall of the main sanctuary.*

The Vietnamese occupation from 1979-89, harsh enough in its own way, began the process of reconstruction, but it was hampered however by continual fighting with the Khmer Rouge who occupied the frontier areas, supported (let it not be forgotten) by American and Chinese equip-

9 *The entrance to the main sanctuary. The main image of Avalokiteśvara which stood inside, has been taken to the National Museum in Phnom Penh. Ta Prohm (Kandal) is the best preserved and maintained temple-fortress which I have seen anywhere in Cambodia.*

10 *The summit shrine of Chao Srei Ribol, a much ruined temple-fortress constructed around a hill, which is walled all around. It lies some twenty kms east of Angkor and well represents the state of dereliction of so many other ancient Khmer sites throughout Cambodia.*

ment and arms. Barely ten years have passed since the UNO appeared on the scene with the good intentions of putting all things to rights. Even so, only since 1998 have the last of the Khmer Rouge been induced to surrender to the present government and the whole country become reasonably safe for travel. However we should now turn from the present to the past.

11 Phnom Chisor, some 70 kms south of Phnom Penh. Such low solitary flat hills (phnom) presented themselves as well suited for Khmer temple-fortresses.

12 It is in a much ruined condition but preserves some fine stone carvings on several of its lintels.

13 A Theravâdin monastery has been built close to the ruins and thus this site has become a popular place of pilgrimage.
This elegantly built temple probably dates from 19th-20th century.

14 *Kampong Saom on the SW coast is Cambodia's main port.*

15 *Kampong Saom also has some fine beaches set around the promontary. Some are decorated with modern statues of classical design, mainly drawn from the Râmâyana, in this case the figures of monkey-chief Hanuman being carried by the sea-goddess "Golden Fish" (pâli: Suvannamaccha).*

NOTE ON TRANSLITERATION AND PRONUNCIATION

These should cause no trouble to most readers and the notes that follow serve mainly as an apology to oriental scholars, who may light upon this work and readily note its spelling deficiencies. However, the general reader should note that the letter c is regularly soft in many languages and never hard as in 'cat'. Thus not only in Sanskrit, but also in Indonesian, Cambodian, etc, c is pronounced as a light (unaspirated) ch, almost as in English 'cheese'. To indicate this sound in terms of Sanskrit derivation I use the symbol ç. Thus vajrâçàrya, "tantric master" is pronounced vajràchârya. Vairocana, the Supreme Buddha, is pronounced as Vairòchana with accent on the second syllable. For well established names, e.g. Cham, Champa, I retain this popularized spelling.

Other diacritical marks in the writing of Sanskrit names and terms are limited to those immediately available on my computer. The three sibilants are thus distinguished as s, ś and sh, but these cause no special problem to those unacquainted with this language, who need only pronounce the palatal letter ś as a lightly pronounced sh as in the word 'ship'. By contrast, the cerebral sh is pronounced further back in the throat as in 'shop'. Typical examples of such Sanskrit sibilants are these:

Sâmkhya, an Indian school of philosophy (for Sanskrit specialists I note that the *anusvâra*, normally a dot indicating the nazalization of a preceding vowel, is not expressly indicated).

Śâkyamuni Buddha,

Śrîvijaya, the great maritime empire,

Sadâśiva, the name of a famous Brahman in Cambodia,

Bhaishajyaguru, the Buddha of Medicine,

Vishnu, the great god, and *kosthâgara*, a treasury.

From these few examples it may be noted that the circumflex accent marks a long vowel. Also, cerebral letters may be indicated by a change of script to distinguish them from the equivalent dentals in unusual words and in Sanskrit titles, as in *kosthâgara* above and as in *Saddharmapundarîka*, 'The Lotus of the True Law', as translated by H. Kern and B. Nanjio. It would surely be pedantic to note the distinction in the name of Vishnu (as Vishnu) or in Muni, an appellation of Buddha as 'Teacher', and I write nirvâna (not nirvâna), mandala (not mandala) for a sacred circle, and torana (not torana) for an ornamental lintel over a temple entrance, as though they have already been accepted into the English language. The names of the two important Bodhisattvas, Padmapâni and Vajrapâni, also appear without marking the cerebral *n* in -pâni.

The pronunciation of Cambodian (Khmer) creates great difficulties for an outsider, but fortunately all the royal names can be read and pronounced as in Sanskrit, viz. just as they are spelt with the provisos already noted above. They are in fact written thus in Khmer, which uses the same system of writing, but often with differing phonetic values. E.g. Jayavarman, a frequently recurring royal name, is pronounced Jie[k]via[k]-rman by Khmers, where [k] represents a kind of glottal stop. This is, however, of no concern whatsoever to the reader, who can pronounce the name as it appears, namely Ja-ya-varman. The names of the temples are given throughout in a phonetic form, such as Preah Vihear (not Brah Vihâr), the famous temple built on a summit in the Dangrek Mountains, although occasionally different spellings used by others occur in the notes. Place names are given in accordance with acceptable present-day conventions.

CHAPTER 1
THE MARITIME STATE OF FUNAN

South-East Asia emerges into history in the early centuries AD thanks to Chinese accounts found in encyclopaedias, travelogues and dynastic histories. From the 5th century onwards archaeological excavations and the earliest stone inscriptions, normally recording local events in Sanskrit, come to our assistance, and then from the 7th century onwards the traces of significant architectural monuments. For the prehistorical period, namely up to the early centuries AD, one relies exclusively upon sporadic archaeological excavations and surmise. Apart from the aborigines who lived (and still live) in remote jungle areas, settled communities would seem to have been generally of two kinds. There were those who lived inland, leading a settled agricultural life, and those who lived by the sea, developing ports in suitable places and thus a flourishing maritime trade.[5] Thanks to the far-flung trade-routes that connected the Roman and Chinese empires via the Malay peninsula and archipelago, as well as the coastal ports of Indo-China, cosmopolitan city-states in certain strategic positions became pre-eminent. It is in such cities as these that Indian religious and cultural influences soon began to affect the predominantly Malay population.

The earliest information concerning these places comes from Chinese accounts. In the mid-3rd century an embassy was despatched by the King of Wu (the southernmost of the Chinese states following upon the break-up of China at the fall of the Han Dynasty in 220) to the kingdom known by the Chinese as Funan, which at that time appears to have been the most powerful maritime state in the "Southern Seas". The original reports of this embassy have disappeared but parts are preserved as quotations in

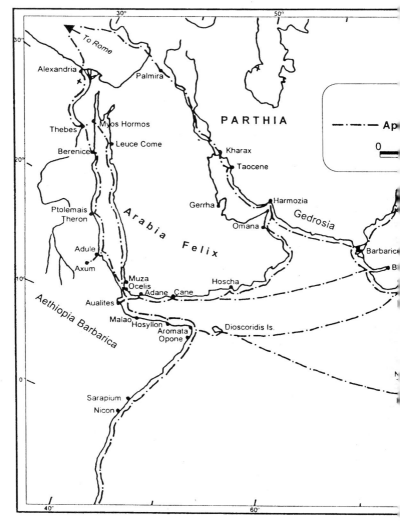

Map 1 *Trade routes from the Mediterranean to the East, First Century AD.*

Source: this map of Paul Wheatley (*The GoldenKersonese p. 282*) is based on information in the *The Periplus of the Erythraean Sea* (Hakluyt Society, London, 1980) and the Ch'ien Han Shu (*Annals of the Former Han Dynasty, 206 BD to AD 8*).

the works of later Chinese writers. I quote from the indispensable work of Paul Wheatley, *The Golden Khersonese*, a passage preserved in the 6th-century *Annals of the Liang Dynasty* concerning the King of Funan.

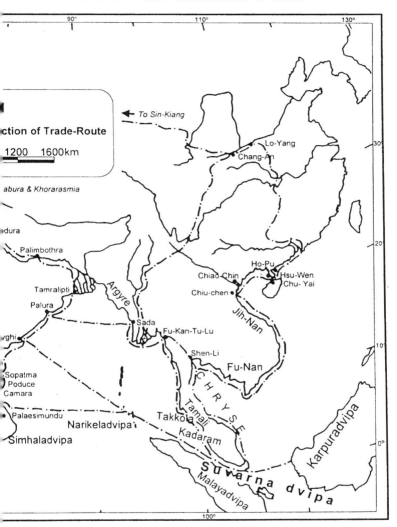

Once more he used troops to attack and subdue the neighbouring kingdoms, which all acknowledged themselves as his vassals. He himself adopted the title of Great King of Funan. Then he ordered the construction of great ships and crossing right over the Chang-hai, attacked more than ten kingdoms, including Chü-tu-k'un, Chiu-chih and Tien-sun. He extended his kingdom for 5-6,000 li. Then he attacked the kingdom of Chin-lin.

The king referred to was named Fan-man and he came to the throne at the beginning of the 3rd century. Paul Wheatley identifies the *Chang-hai* as the Gulf of Siam, *Chin-lin* as a state on the same gulf, and the three other named places as ports along the Malay Peninsula (*op.cit.*, pp.14-25). It is now well established that Funan was situated on the south-west coast of Indo-China corresponding to the southern part of present-day Cambodia and extending into the southern tip of Vietnam. Excavations and aerial photography reveal that there was once here an important trade emporium at Oc Eo (close to modern Rach Gia). Photography reveals a pattern of rectilineal canals, linking the Bassac River to the sea. Towns lay inland close to their cultivated land, which ships could approach by way of the canal system.[6] The cumbersome form of Chinese transliteration of local place-names not only obscures the actual local place-name, as indeed in the case of Funan, but also makes their identification unusually difficult. Since my intention here is merely to give an impression of the general situation existing throughout this whole area in the early centuries AD, this is not a problem which need concern us greatly here.

It is noteworthy that the city-states which gradually developed along the Thai-Malay peninsula are found for the most part on the eastern side, possibly because the land is more open and fertile there but also because of the relative proximity of Funan, which encouraged trade and shipping across the Gulf of Siam. One of the earliest of such city-states to be mentioned by the Chinese is that of Pan-pan, which flourished during the 5th and 6th centuries in the region of the Isthmus of Kra, in the area of (later) Chaiya. The earliest mention of it (in the *Annals of the Liang Dynasty*, 502-57) brings it directly into relationship with Funan.

Chiao Chen-ju (Kaundinya) was originally an Indian Brahman who received a divine fiat to reign over Funan. Chiao Chen-ju rejoiced in his heart. He arrived in Pan-pan to the southward. When the Funanese heard of him, they all welcomed him with delight, went before him and chose him as their king. Once more he modified all the laws to confirm with the usage of India.

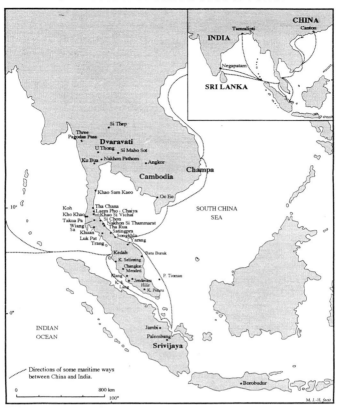

Map 2 *The Malay peninsula and some of its archaeological sites.*
By courtesy of Michel Jacq-Hergoualc'h (see Bibliography).

Pan-Pan is described in several later Chinese compilations:

The people live mostly by the water-side, and in default of city-walls
erect palisades of wood. The king reclines on a golden dragon-couch,
with all his chief retainers kneeling before him, their hands crossed
and resting on their shoulders. In the country are numerous brahmans
who have come from India in search of wealth. They are in high
favour with the king. There are ten monasteries where Buddhist monks
and nuns study their canon.[7]

Another important city-state on the east coast of the Thai-
Malay peninsula is Nakhon Si Thammarat, known in the earlier period as Tâmbralinga (written *Tan-ma-ling* in Chinese).

The ruler of the kingdom of Tan-ma-ling is called Hsiang Kung (lit.
= Minister of State). Around the city there is a wooden pallisade six
or seven feet thick and over twenty feet high, which can be used (as a
platform) for fighting. The inhabitants of the country ride buffaloes,

knot their hair behind and go bare-footed. For their houses the offi-
cials use wood while the common people built bamboo huts with leaf
partitions and rattan buildings. Indigenous products include bee's wax,
lakawood, ghariwood, ebony, camphor, ivory, and rhinoceros horn.
Foreign (merchants) traffic in pongee parasols and umbrellas, skeins
of Ho-ch'ih silk, wine, rice, salt, sugar, porcelain vessels, earthen-
ware bowls and similar coarse and heavy wares, together with gold
and silver platters.[8]

As for the eventual predominance of Funan, I quote a
passage concerning *Tun-sun*, alias Tien-sun, following as
above Paul Wheatley's suggested translation:

More than 3,000 li from the southern frontier of Funan is the king-
dom of Tun-sun, which is situated on an ocean stepping stone. The
land is 1,000 li in extent, the city is 10 li from the sea. There are five
kings who all acknowledge themselves vassals of Funan. The eastern
frontier of Tun-sun is in communication with Chiao-chou
(Tongking), the western with T'ien-chu (India) and An-hsi
(Parthia). All the countries beyond the frontier come and go in pur-
suit of trade, because Tun-sun curves round and projects into the sea
for more than a thousand li. The Chang-hai (Gulf of Siam) is of
great extent and ocean-going junks have not yet crossed it direct. At
this point East and West meet together so that daily there are innu-
merable people there. Precious goods and rare merchandise – there is
nothing that is not there (op.cit., p.16).

6

As is generally admitted, such passages cause problems
not only in translation but also in interpretation. The no-
tion of "an ocean stepping stone" and the statement that
Tun-sun had an eastern frontier, whence China was
reached, and a western one towards India, suggests that
the name refers to a collection of five petty kingdoms strad-
dling the isthmus of the Malay Peninsula. On the peninsula's eastern side ships would be bound to cross the Gulf
of Siam in order to reach Funan. Thus the statement that
the *Chang-hai* is of great extent and ocean-junks have not
yet crossed it direct may mean in this context that it was
still considered dangerous to make the longer sea-journey
right around the Malay Peninsula crossing the South China
Sea so far south of the Gulf of Siam. There is no doubt
that these several city-states, often of uncertain identification, the lesser ones on the west and the major ones on
the east coast of the Malay Peninsula, continued to flourish because of the necessary land-transport from one coast

to the other. The land journey normally took ten days, but
with the general improvement in shipping and greater
knowledge of climatic conditions, especially the periods
of the monsoon winds, the longer sea-route gradually came
to be preferred.

Funan maintained its great maritime empire well into
the 6th century, becoming at the same time an important
centre for the propagation of Buddhist teachings, received
from the Indian side via the Malay Peninsula and trans-
mitted eastwards to the maritime state of Champa on the
east coast of Indo-China, as well as to the Chinese court.
As for Champa, inscriptions dating from perhaps the early
5th century refer to the foundation of a Śaivite temple at
Mi-son, while the presence of Buddhism is attested by the
famous Dong-duong Buddha (now in the National Museum of Saigon). The cult of Avalokiteśvara seems to have
prevailed in this early period, as elsewhere in South-East
Asia. In AD 875 a large monastery was founded, dedicated
to Lakshmîndra Avalokiteśvara, at Dong-duong by King
Indravarman II, in his capital named Indrapura.[9] This is
the largest Buddhist monastery of which such extensive
remains survive in the whole of South-East Asia, recalling
such sites as Sarnath in the Ganges Valley.

As for Funan, there is reference to Buddha-images and
a stûpa in ivory sent to the Chinese court, and certainly
from the 5th century onwards monks were engaged in the
task of assisting with translations from Sanskrit into Chinese, although the royal court of Funan was probably more
interested in Brahmanical traditions. Funan is much praised
by the Chinese for its high standard of culture, but in the
second half of the 6th century it finally succumbed to the
attacks of the inland-based kingdoms of the Khmers to
the north. This resulted in the disintegration of its maritime empire, thus leaving the way open for a new maritime empire to develop, namely that of Śrîvijaya.

One gains the impression that all these early city-states
on the east coast of the Thai-Malay peninsula develop and
thrive in the first place as the result of trading ventures,
primarily between India and Funan, which make use of

the overland routes available across the "neck" of the peninsula. Originally independent of Funan, they gradually
come within the orbit of the Funanese maritime empire.
Only as trading vessels gain greater confidence in taking
the longer sea-route through the Straits of Malacca, thus
rejecting the overland route, does an important city-state
such as Kedah become pre-eminent on the western coast
of the peninsula. With the fall of Funan under repeated
Khmer attacks in the 6th and 7th centuries, the longer
sea-route gains in importance, resulting in the creation of
the Srîvijayan Empire with its main emporiums on the
south-east coast of Sumatra. Thus the earlier city-states
along the Thai-Malay peninsula are released from Funanese
suzerainty, becoming in due course subject to Srîvijaya from
the 7th century onwards. Later in the 12th to 13th centuries
the Khmer empire at its greatest extent, reaching far down
the Thai-Malay peninsula, finds itself in contact with
Srîvijaya. This however was at the time that both empires,
the maritime one and the land one were gradually losing
their outlaying dependencies.

For a brief account of the history of Srîvijaya, see my
Asian Commitment, Ch. X.

CHAPTER 2
THE KHMERS

The Khmers are among the earliest historically known people of mainland South-East Asia, occupying the whole middle and lower Mekong Valley. Others, often at war with the Khmers, were the Chams, who occupied the eastern coastal areas (much of present-day Vietnam), the Mons, who occupied what is now central Thailand (around the Gulf of Siam), and the Pyus, who occupied central Burma. Such was the situation in the early centuries AD when the first historical documentation, primarily carved stone inscriptions (5th century onwards), become available. The Vietnamese, who finally vanquished the Chams, the Thais, who overran the Mons and who pressed mercilessly on the Khmer kingdom, and the Burmese, who absorbed both the Mons and the Pyus, all arrived later on the scene and their southward advance can be followed with fair precision.

9

Like the later arrivals, the Khmers, Mons, Chams and Pyus may have descended in the prehistoric period (no approximate dates can be given) mainly from the high river-valleys which cut through eastern Tibet and southwest China. I would surmise, judging only by facial resemblances, that all these groups have a common racial origin, to which the rather unsatisfactory term Mongoloid is usually given. It may also be reasonable to assume that their various languages derive from a single hypothetical parent language. It is already possible to talk hypothetically of Sino-Tibetan languages, divided into the two main groups of Tibeto-Burman languages, to which the Pyu language surely belongs, and Sino-Thai, which comprise Chinese dialects, Thai and maybe Vietnamese, although it appears to have features which may link it to the Mon-Khmer group. All these named languages have some literary history, which provides the only means of investigating sound changes back into the past, but there are many other pockets of related languages spoken today throughout the more mountainous areas which have no literary history at all.

Chinese was being written as early as 1000 BC in the form of inscriptions on bones and shells, but it was not until the 3rd century BC that the system was standard-

16 Phnom Da at Angkor Borei, an ancient hill-top Śaivite temple. Angkor Borei, situated some 45 kms south-east of Takeo, is probably the site of the ancient capital of Funan. Excavations sponsored by the University of Hawii and the Royal University of Fine Arts are even now underway.

17 The west side of this same early brick-built temple, probably 6th -7th century.

ised, and as the characters are basically non-phonetic, although often used as phonetic elements, the fixing of the actual earlier pronunciation of words has proved a laborious task. Inscriptions in Mon (as well as in Pâli), dating from the 6th century and maybe earlier, are found in the ancient Mon Buddhist civilization of Dvâravatî, as known from excavated sites throughout present-day central Thailand.[10] Writing is known in Tibet from the 7th century and inscriptions in stone, found in the Yarlung Valley (south-east of Lhasa), are well attested from the 8th century. Khmer appears on various inscriptions also from the 7th century onwards, accompanying inscriptions in San-

18 *The small museum at Angkor Borei in its attractive river-side setting. Most of the images there are copies, as the originals have been taken to the national museum in Phnom Penh, where they may more easily be seen.*

skrit, which is attested in Indo-China from at least the 5th century onwards. Written Burmese is attested from the 11th century onwards. Thai does not emerge as a written language until the 13th century. These are very short periods indeed in terms of the hundreds of thousands of years of the development and change of languages throughout this area, and the means are lacking for tracing their earlier associations, just as the place or places of origin of human language itself inevitably remain unknown.

The assumption that the Khmers and the other historically identifiable inhabitants of the Indo-Chinese mainland all came from further north does not imply that they arrived in areas devoid of indigenous peoples, such as those classed by anthropologists as "Veddoid" (because of a presumed relationship with the known Veddas of Ceylon). Doubtless such early races survive in the remoter parts of the Malay archipelago, while their presence on the scene when the Malays arrived in gradual waves, travelling largely down the Malay peninsula but also arriving by sea, certainly resulted in the usual human mixing of the species.[11] The tendency to racial mixture is world-wide, and it certainly applied to the Mon-Khmers when several thousand years ago they began to settle the territories which they occupy today. Such racial mixture continues into recent times and much of commerce and business throughout Cambodia is in the hands of Khmers of mixed Chinese origin, who speak only Khmer and no longer Chinese. There are Khmers of Cham origin, and doubtless Khmers of Thai origin, although the numbers of "Thais" of Khmer origin, who now speak only Thai, must be far more numerous, since Thailand now occupies so much of the territory which was once Khmer. Then again there are the "Khmers" of the south-eastern part of the old Khmer kingdom, which belongs to modern Vietnam, who now speak only Vietnamese. Thus generally one can define as Khmer anyone who speaks Khmer as his home language, whatever his racial origin, totally forgotten where the distant past in concerned, but still remembered in the modern period.

The Khmers first enter history in their relationship with Funan, when they appear as the rulers of an inland kingdom, or kingdoms, under the suzerainty of Funan, often with family relationships between the royal families on both sides. As an independent kingdom which won its freedom from Funan during the second half of the 6th century, it was known as Chenla by the Chinese, who record the events in the *Sui Shu* (Annals of the Sui Dynasty, AD 581-618).

Near the capital of the kingdom is a mountain named Ling-chia-po-p'o (= Lingaparvata, viz. Wat Phu), on the summit of which a temple was constructed, always guarded by a thousand soldiers and consecrated to the spirit named P'o-to-li (viz. Bhadreśvara), to whom human sacrifices are made. Each year the king himself goes to this temple to make a human sacrifice during the night.

Thus the capital of this kingdom, known as Śresthapura, probably named after a king Śresthavarman (son of Śrutavarman), seems to have been situated near Wat Phu, now in the far south of Laos near Champasak.[12] In any case, it was later regarded as the source of the Khmer monarchy, since Jayavarman VII in an inscription of 1186 AD is praised as "a descendent of Śrutavarman and Śresthavarman, the origins of a brilliant line of kings".[13] This was also the solar dynasty deriving from the mythical marriage between the Sage Kambu Svâyambhuva and the celestial nymph Merâ.[14] The reference to human sacrifice by the Khmers has later associations, for it was still being performed in the 19th century on the summit of Ba Phnom (some 60 kilometres south-east of Phnom Penh). The sacrifice was offered to Durgâ (consort of Śiva) in the manifestation of "Slayer of the Buffalo-Demon" (*Mahîshâsuramardini*), who was also popular in East Java. David Chandler's informant, an old man who witnessed the last occasion of such a sacrifice, told him that only prisoners already condemned to death for a serious crime were chosen as victims and that their consent to die as a form of sacrifice was seemingly required.[15] Ba Phnom may have been an important strategic and sacred site for the people of Funan before it was occupied by the Khmers (see the following note). The possibility suggests itself that this was a very ancient rite, confirming their victory over Funan, just as the earlier sacrifice on Wat Phu may well have confirmed their victory over the Chams.

This occupation of the capital city of Funan, known as T'e-mu by the Chinese, was achieved by a king named Bhavavarman and his cousin Çitrasena (who later ruled as Mahendravarman) in the second half of the 6th century.[16] Bhavavarman, whose capital was Bhavapura, was himself

13

related to the royal family of Funan, with the result that later Khmer kings sometimes attributed the origin of their line to Rudravarman, the last king of Funan, thus also appropriating the dynastic legend of the founding of Funan as the result of a marriage between the Brahman Kaundinya and a *nâgi*, a variant of the same myth noted above.

According to Chinese sources, the final conquest of Funan was achieved in the first half of the 7th century by the son of Mahendravarman, Îśânavarman, who built a new capital for himself, known as Îśânapura, a site now known as Sambor Prei Kuk, buried in the jungle 32 kilometres north of Kampong Thom. During my two visits to

19 *Khmer brick-built temples of the early 7th century. They form part of the ancient Khmer capital of Îśânapura, now known as Sambor Prei Kuk, a complex of Śaivite shrines in the jungle some 32 kms north of Kampong Thom. This city was founded by King Îśânavarman (possible dates approximately 615-635) following upon the final defeat of Funan by the Khmers. The decorative brickwork reproduces the motif of the same type of shrine in miniature.*

this site (April 1997 and February 1998), I was astounded at the ambitious layout of this ancient royal city, which prefigures the later capital at Angkor. There are innumerable brick-built temples, each a square brick shrine on a raised platform and surmounted by a tiered brick roof. Thanks to earlier French efforts for the preservation these temples, they retain much of their original decorative brick-work, not only decorative devices, but also plaques illustrating divinities and human figures. A Sanskrit inscription refers to the setting up of a Śiva-linga in the Śaka year 549 (AD 627) by a high official, a Pâśupâta Brahman, who was versed in grammar, the Brahmanical systems of Vaiseshika, Nyâya and Sâmkhya, and the doctrine of the Sugata (the Buddha).[17]

There are three main groups of temples. The one to the north, the most extensive, seems now so dispersed in the jungle that its configuration is difficult to define. That to the south, still standing within its square enclosure, is certainly an impressive site. One enters from the east, passing a subsidiary temple, which contains a finely worked miniature stone shrine, now empty. It was perhaps intended for a special image of Nandin, Śiva's sacred bull, although it seems unusually elaborate for such a purpose. Immediately ahead is the central temple of Śiva with a remarkably high pinnacled roof, rising in a steep ascent of carefully corbelled brick-work; it can be best appreciated by gazing upwards from the empty interior. To each of the four intermediate quarters there stands an octagonal temple, the like of which I have not seen at Angkor.[18] A smaller seemingly ill-defined group of shrines lies in a west-central direction.

15

Although this important site of Sambor Prei Kuk, well to the south, provides the most impressive examples of early Khmer architecture, rather more modest shrines, also dating to the mid-7th century, were already being built in the Dangrek Mountains, which at that time seem to have represented the northern limits of Khmer influence (see pp. 39-40).

This first Khmer kingdom, of which we have substantial archaeological remains, had no lack of building skills,

20 *The lower section of a square-built brick shrine at Sambor Prei Kuk, showing the ornamental water-spout (*somasûtra*) and a section of decorative brick-work, probably showing palace-scenes.*

no lack of manpower to carry out such works, and no lack of wealth, which could surely only derive from agriculture and animal husbandry. It is interesting to contrast it with Funan, whose power and wealth depended primarily on its maritime trade, and thus comprised a cosmopolitan populace in its main port and presumably also in its capital. Funan was fully receptive to Indian cultural and religious influences, and such influences as reached the Khmers in their inland strongholds presumably reached them through their contacts (including inter-marriage) with Funan. One should not, however, conceive of the inland Khmers as devoid of higher material culture up to the arrival of certain cultural and religious traditions from far-away India.

It has been known for a long time that the so-called Dongsong culture flourished in the valley of the Red River (Tongking), now in northern Vietnam, during the early centuries BC. It has been named after a village where most of the items were found, namely: weapons, utensils in bronze, decorative devices of bone and shell, and especially the famous bronze "thunder drum", which had a widespread influence throughout South-East Asia. These Dongsong sites date back to about 500 BC and were productive for five to six hundred years until the occupation of the region by the Chinese.[19]

More recent excavations in north-western Thailand have revealed the existence of high cultural levels of material life, dating back from several thousand years ago up to the early centuries BC. Most of the items have been found in places of burial, namely weapons and ornaments,

21 *This same motif, probably of royal figures, in often set in an elaborate framework, suggestive of a palace. It appears frequently on these early 7th century temples, and since it has no sustaining framework, it is sometimes referred to as a "flying palace". It is doubtful if its creators conceived of it as flying.*

or sections of them, worked in bronze, beads and patterned bangles and decorative pottery. Numerous examples of such artefacts may be seen in the Bangkok National Museum, and elsewhere in local museums, especially at Lopburi, Khorat, Phimai, Ubon Ratchathani and Khon Kaen. Efforts have been made to deduce the state of agriculture and husbandry, and it is now known that rice was a staple food at least over 5,000 years ago.[20] There were no Thais yet in these regions in this remote period, and among the most likely local inhabitants of these sites were surely Mon-Khmers. It is impossible that the Khmers, whom we hear of in the early centuries AD, were not profoundly affected by these material developments. The essential extras were contact with Indian culture and religion, resulting in the creation of a literary language and new forms of imagery and temple construction. One must presume that the same kind of local cultural basis was equally valid for Funan, to which were added the more luxurious items of maritime trade, as well as the religious and literary culture of India.

According to the *Liang Shu* (Annals of the Liang Dynasty, 502-57) the capital of Funan was 500 li (200 kilometres) from the sea,[21] probably meaning the great maritime emporium at Oc Eo near Rach Gia (South Vietnam), where excavations and aerial photography have been carried out (see note 6 above). As the map distance in a straight line is 150 kilometres, this would seem to be factually true. One notes also that Wat Phu, the presumed capital of the Khmer ruler Mahendravarman, is 400 kilometres in a straight line from the capital of Funan, which was overrun by his son Îsânavarman. The victor's new capital of Îsânapura (Sambor Prei Kuk) is close on 150 kilometres in a straight line from the Funan capital which he now occupied. Thus he brought his centre of power much further to the south. As his conquests also extended beyond the Great Lake (Tonle Sap), this confederation of petty states may have been quite as large as present-day Cambodia. Îsânavarman had no interest in assuming control of Funan's far reaching maritime empire, for which he surely lacked the means and the ability. This disintegrated, only to be regrouped as the maritime empire of Śrīvijaya, but local ports would have continued to function. Apart from the trophies of war, he may seem to have lost far more than he gained: an unwieldy kingdom, of which the southern section was deprived of its primary source of wealth, and where opposition to his rule from Funan's royal successors was only to be expected. The changes which now occurred also seem to have resulted in some temporary persecution of Buddhism, according to I-tsing, who sailed from Canton in AD 671 for India. He mentions first Lin-yi (closely associated with Champa in Chinese sources) with seeming approbation, and then mentions Funan:

Setting out westwards (from Lin-yi), one reaches (on foot) within a month the country (Kuo) of Poh-nan, formerly called Fu-nan. Of old it was a country, the inhabitants of which lived naked; the people were mostly worshippers of heaven (the gods or devas), but later on Buddhism flourished there, but a wicked king has now expelled and exterminated them all, and there are no members of the Buddhist brotherhood at all, while adherents of other religions (or heretics) live intermingled.[22]

19

As hearsay, one need scarcely treat this as a final word on the subject, but one notes that whereas Funan was primarily interested in Buddhism up to the time of its overthrow, the Khmer kings whom we have met so far were only interested in the cult of Śiva, and there may have been persecution in some areas. In any case, it proved impossible for the successors of Îśânavarman to hold the country together, namely Bhavavarman II and Jayavarman I, followed by his daughter Queen Jayadevî, who is mentioned in an inscription dated 713.

Thus, already from the beginning of the 8th century, the Chinese begin to refer to a Lower ("Water") Chenla and an Upper ("Land") Chenla. Upper Chenla, probably comprising what is now northern Cambodia, the lower Mun Valley around present-day Ubon Ratchathani and southern Laos, may have held together at least until the reign of Jayadevî. Lower Chenla, presumably corresponding more or less to Funan, namely the lower Mekong valley, split up as the result of dynastic feuds.[23] Meanwhile the coastal areas from Tongking southwards, occupied by the Chams who had adopted Indian cultural traditions with seeming enthusiasm, were under assault by the "Jâvakas" of Śrîvijaya. Near Tongking a stone inscription of 767 records this attack and the resultant pillage, while two inscriptions in Champa, dated 774 and 787, record similar invasions. There are no such precise records of invasions on the south (Cambodian) coast, but as this was so much nearer home for the attackers, they are likely to have had a more lasting effect with the actual occupation of limited areas.

Within this context there may be some truth in a strange "seaman's tale". A 10th-century Arab writer, Abu Zaid Hassan, retells a story attributed to the merchant Sulayman about how the Mahârâja of Zâbag (Śrîvijaya) retaliated against the threat of a Khmer king by sending an expedition to cut off this king's head and bring it to him on a dish. "When the news of these events reached the kings of India and China, the Mahârâja became even greater in their eyes. From that moment the Khmer kings, every morning upon rising, turned their faces in the direction of the country of Zâbag, bowed down to the ground and humbled themselves before the Mahârâja to render him homage."[24] There seems to be some substance to this story, for the king who restored some unity to the Khmer kingdom in the early 9th century considered it necessary at his consecration to perform a special Brahmanical ritual to ensure that the Khmers should be no longer be subject to "Java".

20

The story of this 9th-century king, Jayavarman II, is known from an 11th-century stele inscription found on the site of a Khmer temple originally known as Bhadraniketana, in Aranyaprathet Province (Thailand). This is now just beyond the limits of the present western frontier of Cambodia, but in the 11th century this place lay on the main route linking Angkor to the recent Khmer acquisitions around the Gulf of Siam. This important inscription, known as the Sdok Kak Thom stele, is now kept in the Bangkok Museum.[25] It was set up in 1052 during the reign of King Udayâdityavarman II (see below) to commemorate the foundation by a distinguished Brahman, named Sadâśiva, of a temple at this place containing a "personal *linga*" known as *Jayendravarmeśvara* (Victorious Indra Lord of Protection). Sadâśiva had been "priest" (*purohita*) to the previous King Sûryavarman (1002-50), but he had renounced his celibacy in order to marry the sister-in-law of the king himself. The text traces his "lineage" back to the Brahman Śivakaivalya, who had been the priest of Jayavarman II and who was associated with the institution of the ritual of the *Devarâja* (God-King) in the first half of the 9th century. This essential ritual had been performed by a specially qualified Brahman named Hiranyadâma. Thus this new shrine contained images of Hiranyadâma and of Śivakaivalya-Śivâśrama "equal in majesty to Brahma and Vishnu-Śiva". (Śivâśrama was the predecessor of Sadâśiva, and was thus associated with Śivakaivalya, the combination of names representing the beginning and end of the spiritual lineage up to that time.)

The inscription is primarily interested in the new shrine and its incredibly rich endowments, as well as in the Brahmanical lineage of these privileged high-priests, solely authorized to perform the *devarâja* (God-King) ritual. The story of how this primary event occurred results incidentally in a brief account of Jayavarman's life story. Apart from the eulogistic language, the events are related in a strictly factual manner with no hint of explanation. "For the prosperity of the people he arose like the new blossoming of a large stemless lotus-flower in this perfectly pure lineage of kings". Thus his origins are uncertain, although he may have been an important member of one of the royal families of Lower Chenla. Speculating further, one can suggest that he might have been a local ruler, carried off in captivity, with the result that on his return he had a base from which to embark upon his victorious progress. Even his original name is unknown, since Jayavarman is the royal name assumed at his coronation, maybe in the year 802. We learn that "His Majesty came from Java in order to rule in the city of Indrapura". Thus the text suggests a triumphant return from exile, although his subsequent changes of residence suggest rather that he needed to win his way to power stage by stage. Indrapura seems to be reliably identifed as Bantay Prei Nokor on the outskirts of Kampong Cham.

It would be a long way from "Java" to here and nothing is known of the circumstances of the journey. Also while there is no absolute certainty to whichever part of Java or Sumatra or even the Malay Peninsula "Java" may refer, it is sometimes readily assumed that the Central Java of the Śailendra kings is intended, where the great stûpa of Borobudur was even then in the process of construction. But if one considers that this "Java" whence he came was an aggressive power from which he was resolved to free his country in accordance with his later coronation ritual, it could scarcely refer to the 8th-9th century inland Śailendra Kingdom of Central Java. It could more reasonably be applicable to Śrîvijaya, which was the only power at that time capable of maintaining a form of suzerainty over southern Cambodia. Some confirmation of this derives from the Arab name for Śrîvijaya, namely Zâbag (a name deriving precisely from "Jâvaka").[26] It may be significant that Jayavarman arrived in Cambodia as a confirmed Śaivite, like previous Khmer kings, seemingly antagonistic to the fervent Buddhism of Śrîvijaya and Central Java.

In Bantay Prei Nokor (Indrapura), where Jayavarman first established himself, there are impressive ruins of a doubly walled temple of the pre-Angkor period, in the centre of which a Theravâdin *vihâra* has been skilfully constructed.[27] (It recalled to my mind the great mosque of Cordoba, in the centre of which the Spanish conquerors constructed their cathedral church; however, this Cambodian equivalent presents a much more harmonious combination.) Thus Indrapura would have been the capital of a local ruler when Jayavarman arrived. What might have been their relationship? It seems certain that Jayavarman became effectively master of the place. Here he became associated with a Brahman scholar named Śivakaivalya, who was already established seemingly as the leading Brahman in Indrapura, responsible for an hereditary shrine con-

22 Bantay Prei Nokor in the vicinity of Kampong Cham. This is an ancient Śaivite temple-fortress, identified as the citadel of Indrapura, where Jayavarman II, arrived from "Java" towards the end of the 8th century on the first stage of his seemingly triumphant return to Cambodia. It is one of the several important sites which was adapted as a Theravâdin monastery in the 16th century or maybe even earlier, as can be clearly seen from the protruding roof of Thai-Khmer-style Vat, as also by the pinnacled tower just behind.

taining a Śiva-linga. This Brahman followed him on subsequent journeys and together they moved perhaps along the east side of the Great Lake, where Jayavarman bestowed upon his Brahman companion a village and a territory known as Kuti. The king then proceeded to establish himself at Hariharâlaya, present-day Ruluos. Now well known to tourists, Ruluos is some 15 kilometres from Siem Reap, going south along the road east of the lake which leads eventually to Kampong Thom. Some 45 kilometres further south of Ruluos along this same route is the town of Kampong Kdei, through which the king and his Brahman companion must have passed. This small town on the Chikreng River remains remarkable for its massive stone Angkor-style bridge with its *nâga* railings and *nâgas* with raised hoods at both ends of the causeway. This suggests that it was a fief of some importance; this particular place named Kdei is a more likely identification for the Kuti bestowed upon the Brahman Śivakaivalya than Bantay Kdei within the confines of Angkor, as was first suggested by Coedès and has often been repeated. The Brahman

23 The impressive Angkor-style bridge, 80 metres long and 12
metres wide, at Kampong Kdei, a small town some 60 kms south of
Siem Reap along the road which passes east of the Great Lake on
the way to Kampong Thom. It was reconstructed in the 1960s.

24

continued to serve the king at Hariharâlaya until they
moved on and "founded" the city of Amarendrapura, now
usually identified as a site with ancient ruins, notably Prâsâd
Ak Yom by the south side of the Western Baray (Angkor).

The construction of this great reservoir two centuries
later resulted in their interment, and thus the labour of
disinterring them completely is practically impossible owing to the presence of the lake immediately above. Since
dates as early as 609 and 704 have been identified on this
site, Jayavarman can scarcely have founded a city here,
but the author of the text on the stele may have thought
so, or else the site of Amarendrapura is not yet identified
with certainty. It would seem that all the places so far visited must have been former "cities" of local Khmer rulers,
whom Jayavarman won over to his cause. Here at
Amarendrapura the Brahman Śivakaivalya received more
territory and he arranged for members of his family from
Kuti to come and take charge of these new estates.

Then he and Jayavarman next went to
Mahendraparvata (the Mountain of Mighty Indra), namely
Phnom Kulen, about 30 kilometres north-east of Angkor

24 Ak Yom, all that remains of the earliest known "temple-mountain" in the whole Angkor area. A three-tier structure built mainly of brick, it is dedicated to Śiva under the name of Gambhîreśvara, with inscribed dates of 609, 704 and 1001 recording work done on the site. It was subsequently buried during the second half of the 11th century under the south embankment of the Western Baray as constructed by Udayâdityavarman (1050-66), and even now the total excavation of the site remains impracticable.

25

(some 70 kilometres by road) in order to perform the consecration ritual, already referred to above. Phnom Kulen is the major south-eastern escarpment of a high broken sandstone plateau, its highest points ranging from 400 to 500 metres and thus dominating the Angkor plain to the south.[28] The southern summit, which looks towards Angkor, was the centre of a large number of brick-built temples and stone shrines, resembling those at Sambor Prei Kuk, and these presumably represented the city founded by Jayavarman. Other similar shrines are located over a wide area that from the available sketch-map appears to cover a range of some 20 kilometres east to west and some 30 kilometres to the north and north-east. The neighbouring north-western section of the plateau, which rises to about 300 metres, is the source of the Siem Reap River and its tributary, the Ruisey (Bamboo) stream, which flow towards Angkor, supplying water for its (earlier) many artificial lakes and moats. It was regarded as a sacred river at

25-26 Stone carvings along the upper reaches of the Ruisey
(Bamboo) Stream, a tributary of the Siem Reap River which has its
source on Phnom Kulen. As a sacred source for the replenishment
of the lakes and moats of Angkor, it was adorned with Brahmanical
stone relief carvings along is banks as well as well as under water.

26

25 Carving of Vishnu (as supreme god) giving birth to Brâhma by
means of a lotus stalk issuing from his navel. In the foreground
there is an array of miniature lingas. An inscription records that
Sûryavarman I donated 1,000 such in 1054.

26 In the river-bed one can discern the conventional design of a yoni
with its spout for sacrificial offerings. In its centre there must have
once stood a linga. To the four sides of its emplacement one can
identify four miniature lingas, small rounded bumps, with which
whole stretches of the river are studded.

its source, and thus decorated on the surrounding rocks with carved figures of *lingas*, Hindu divinities, divine attendants and animal figures.[29]

One may presume that it was already known as a sacred mountain and thus presented itself as the suitable place for Jayavarman's consecration. This was performed by a Brahman, Hiranyadâma, of *Janapada*, who instituted this ritual of the "God-King" (*devarâja*) while also initiating the Brahman chaplain Śivakaivalya in the same ritual for future use. Sanskrit *janapada* means "country" and possible "homeland" in this context, indicating that a genuine Brahman had been found for this special occasion.[30] The association of a divinity and by implication a "god-king" with a sacred mountain is so widespread in the ancient Orient that it requires no special comment.

Thus this cult of Khmer kings as *devarâja*, identified with Śiva and symbolized by Śiva's *linga* enshrined on a temple-mountain, was instituted formally by Jayavarman II. The practice was already prefigured by the earlier rites performed at Wat Phu and Ba Phnom, as referred to above. How long he remained at Mount Kulen is unknown, but it was long enough to build a royal city on the southern summit. This appears to have been centred around a form of "temple-mountain", a three-tier shrine, now in a ruined condition, known locally by the inglorious nickname of Rong Chen ("Chinese vegetable-patch").[31] However, it must have been an impressive monument, even larger (the base being 100 metres square) than the Bakong, its immediate successor at Hariharâya (see below). It was almost certainly the main shrine built to receive the first properly consecrated *devarâja*.

27

Continuing with the Sdok Kak Thom inscription, we learn: "Next the King returned to rule in the city of Hariharâlaya and the God-King (*devarâja*, viz. the consecrated *linga*) was also brought, while the high priest and all his relatives officiated as before. The high priest died during this reign. The King died (in 850) in the city of Hariharâlaya where dwelt the God-King (*devarâja*) and this resides in every capital city, wherever taken by successive sovereigns as protector of the kingdom". This inscription seems to presume the existence of one *devarâja* or Royal *linga*, which was set up in the capital wherever Jayavarman II and his successors established themselves. This practice cannot have continued for long owing to the later consecration of personal royal *lingas* by later rulers, as will be seen below.

No inscriptions and no buildings can be identified with certainty from the reigns of Jayavarman II and his son Jayavarman III (850-877) who succeeded him. However, a shrine must surely have been built for the royal *linga* and presumably this was restructured by their successor Indravarman (877-889) to form the magnificent temple-mountain known as the Bakong, which one sees today at Ruluos. It was found as a total ruin and its re-creation under the direction of Maurice Glaize during the years 1936-43 marks it out as perhaps the finest work of French conservation. All that is noticeably missing is the carved friezework, of which only occasional pieces could be traced amongst the ruins.

28

Indravarman's antecedents are unknown, but he may have come from one of the smaller Khmer kingdoms in the south of the country, which was scarcely yet a unified state. One of the first works of his reign was to create a vast artificial lake, known as the *Indratatâka*, for the irrigation of the city, in the middle of which his son and successor Yaśovarman (889-900) built a temple, known as the Lolei (see below), in honour of his parents. Indravarman himself also built the temple known as Preah Ko (Sacred Bull), dedicated to his parents, maternal grand-parents and also to Jayavarman II and his queen, all represented by suitable statues.[32]

What one sees today can give little or no idea of this once magnificent city, watered by canals from the lake which not only supplied the paddy-fields, but which also circulated through the city, around the palace, filling the great moat around the Bakong. Now there is no sign of a lake. The Lolei temple stands high and dry on a ridge, covered with lichen and encumbered with Theravâdin mon-

27 The Preah Ko, also built by Indravarman at Hariharâlaya, is dedicated to his maternal grand-parents, to Jayavarman II and his queen, and to Indravarman's own parents, all represented in this set of six shrines by manifestations of Íiva and his spouse Gauri. The local name "Preah Ko", meaning 'Sacred Bull' relates to the three small statues of Nandin, Íiva's mount, on the east (front) side.

astery buildings which now occupy most of its former court-yard. Alone the Bakong and the Preah Ko (since its re-cent cleaning and repair) stand out as unusual masterpieces.

Preah Ko consists of a set of six brick-built temples of the now traditional design (viz. a square shine containing a small cella, surmounted by a tiered roof) standing on a rectangular platform within a double enclosure. The three front temples, facing east, intended for the male statues, are appreciably larger than the three that stand directly behind, intended for the corresponding female figures. The central shrine to the front is both taller than the other two and skilfully set back, thus emphasising its pre-emi-nence, as though its companions stood forward on guard. They are remarkable for the fine decorative work, espe-cially on the lintels over the entrances and to sides of the doorways where intricate floral motifs, surmounted by the protective mask of *Kâla*, form an elaborate frame for the guardian divinity.[33]

The Bakong, consisting of a slender square temple with pointed tiered roof, raised on a fivefold square terrace, is surely the most elegant of these so-called "temple-mountains". The lower terrace is 65 by 67 metres and the top one 20 by 12; this allows a relatively gentle rise from one terrace to the next. By comparison later "temple-mountains" rise far too steeply from one platform to the next. This serves to emphasize their massiveness, but also results in the summit being obscured from view most of the time as one mounts. The Bakong has a magnificent silhouette from all approaches and all angles. I have seen it suggested that it may have been inspired by Borobudur, but this seems a far-fetched suggestion, the more so as the latter's silhouette is so massive and squat. It resembles Borobudur only in being raised on a series of open terraces with four flights of steps to the four quarters, with an imposing entrance arch at the foot of each flight. But one does not need the great Javanese stûpa as a model for what is effectively the basic design of any monument that affects to represent the mythical central mountain of the universe. Many temples in East Java, notably Çandi Jawi, might serve as a model, if indeed there is need to seek for one.

30

28 *The Bakong, the first great "temple-mountain", built during the reign of King Indravarman (877-889) at Hariharâlaya (Ruluos), the city founded by Jayavarman II in the first half of the 9th century. It was built to enshrine the first Devarâja or "God-King", a Śiva-linga, symbol of royal authority, which had been brought to his new capital by Jayavarman II from Phnom Kulen where he was consecrated king about the year 802. The Bakong was found as a total ruin, and its recreation under the direction of Maurice Glaize during 1936-43 marks it out as one of the finest works of French conservation.*

CHAPTER 3
THE RISE OF ANGKOR

As mentioned above, Indravarman's successor, Yaśovarman, erected the so-called Lolei temple in the middle of the *Indratatâta* lake in honour of his parents.[34] This consists now of four tower-like brick-built shrines in a much ruined condition, two in a row facing south-east with a further two behind. Originally two sets of three shrines must have been intended exactly on the model of Preah Ko. This is suggested immediately by the fact that the two north-eastern shrines, those to the right as one faces the whole complex, are appreciably taller than the other

29 *A fine example of a lintel over a doorway from one of the four remaining shrines of the Lolei. The lintel with Kâla mask, out of which sprout the two coiling ends of a garland, represent the basic design of these Khmer masterpieces, the whole being filled in with a wide choice of subsidiary images. Here one sees a detailed representation of a row of divinities in miniature above and dancing figures interspersed below between the coils of the garland.*

two, and were thus clearly conceived as the central ones. Some finely worked lintels have been preserved, especially the one on the north-eastern tower, which is surmounted by a delicate frieze of a seated Brahmanical sage (Agastya) and other divinities. The site of the two missing towers, possibly never completed, has been cleared as part of the courtyard of the more recent Theravâdin monastery which now presses hard upon these ancient ruins.

Yaśovarman next resolved to create a new city in the vicinity, namely Angkor. Maybe he took this decision because the water supply at Hariharâlaya was no longer adequate for a growing population. In any case, his first great work was the construction of another vast reservoir, named the *Yaśodharatatâka*, 7 by 2 kilometres, to serve the new city. Along the south bank of this vast reservoir he had monasteries (*âsrama*) built for various Hindu religious communities, for Śaivas, Pâsupatas and Tapasvins, Pâñcarâtras, Bhâgavatas and Sâttvatas,[35] and also probably a Buddhist monastery (*Saugatâśrama*), although strangely the stele referring to this was found on the approach to Preah Palilay, built in the 12th century when Buddhism was held in far higher official esteem. Apart from the foundation steles there is now no trace of these buildings, clearly built of less durable materials like the main buildings of the city.

An immediate requirement was a temple-complex suitable to receive the royal *linga*, which presumably should have been transferred in due course to its new abode. This raises the matter of the later practice of individual rulers setting up their own particular "Royal *linga*", a practice not envisaged in the foundation ritual of the "God King" (*devarâja*).[36] If indeed the *Devarâja* were transferred from Hariharâlaya, this would have occasioned the need for a replacement in the original shrine. However, the *linga* in its new location is referred to as *Yasodhareśvara*, "Lord Yaśodhara", suggesting that this was the king's own specially consecrated *linga*, and thus that the *Devarâja* remained in its original home.

For the new temple-mountain he chose the hill known as the Bakheng, which rises steeply on the southern ap-

30 A section of the temple, known as the Lolei, consisting originally of a set of six towers like Preah Ko. It was built by King Yaśovarman and dedicated to his divinized parents, on an island in the middle of the artificial lake, the Indratatâta, a major work of his predecessor Indravarman. The lake has lone since dried up, and the temple stands high and dry on a ridge together with a Theravâdin monastery which takes up most of the surrounding space.

proach to Angkor Thom or "Great Angkor", the new city created by Jayavarman VII in the 12th century, which one sees today. Thus the Bakheng has been effectively marginalized and nowadays it is treated mainly as a fine viewpoint, where tourists gather in large numbers at sunset to see Angkor Vat to the south, the expanse of the Western Baray to the west, and in the distance the summits of Phnom Krom to the south-west and that of Phnom Bok to the north-east. On both of these summits, each of them some 20 kilometres distant, Yaśovarman also built subsidiary shrines. Nowadays the ruins on the summit of

31 The Bakheng, the first temple-mountain to be built at Angkor, crowns a hilltop just to the south of the southern entrance to the later city of Angkor Thom, which has thus effectively marginalized it. Laid out as a mandala, it consists of a central shrine surrounded by four others to the four directions on the summit terrace, surrounded again

the Bakheng give little idea of the magnificent temple-complex as conceived by Yaśovarman and his Brahmanical advisers. The layout is clearly conceived as a mandala. A fivefold terrace, gradually decreasing from 76 metres square at the base to 47 metres at the summit, supports the central terrace on which stood the central shrine with five smaller shrines to the four intermediate quarters. Flights of steps lead up from the four main directions and these were flanked by two rows of five miniature shrines, making a total of 40. Similar single rows of shrines led up from the four intermediate directions, making a total of a fur-

by another 104 smaller shrines, thus making a total of 109. As was clearly the intention, the main central temple dedicated to Śiva is thus surrounded by the sacred number of 108 other shrines, arranged symetrically on a five-tier platform. This was the creation of Yaśovarman, the founder of Angkor, about the year 900.

ther 20, all of these structures so far being built of local sandstone. Around each of the four angles of this enormous complex stood seven brick-built tower-like shrines, making a total of 28, with a double pair of similar shrines at each of the four quarters, a further 16. The total number of these constructions was clearly calculated to arrive at a configuration of one main central shrine surrounded by the sacred number of 108 subsidiary ones. No other temple-mountain approximates to so complex a design, and although the layout of the mandala differs, the great complex of Çandi Sewu in Central Java occurs at once to one's mind as a similar grandiose conception.

By making such comparisons I do not suggest that there need have been any direct cultural influence from Java. A glance at a map is enough to remind one of the considerable distance between the two countries and there is no record of reciprocal official visits or embassies. The only known contact, for what it is worth, is that Jayavarman, who brought some kind of unity to Cambodia in the early 9th century and established the rite of the *Devarâja,* is said to have come from "Java". This is all too readily assumed to be the Central Java of the Śailendra "dynasty", whence he came imbued with Javanese culture, which he thus introduced into the new kingdom, as we read in one of the most authoritative works on the culture of Indo-China.[37]

36

The most likely sources of cultural influences are firstly the Mon (Dvâravatî) communities to the north-west, secondly neighbouring Champa, with which the Khmers were often in direct contact, to the east, and possibly thirdly the several city-states along the east coast of the Thai-Malay peninsula, which in any case were destined to fall eventually under Khmer suzerainty during the 11th century. Regrettably little or nothing now remains above ground of these prosperous Hindu-Buddhist civilizations with which comparisons can usefully be made, except perhaps for the distant Cham sites of Mi-son and Dong-duong in Quang-nam province of Vietnam. However such influences as there might have been were surely occasional and superficial. The basic similarities arise from the related cultural and religious influences from India, which all these various countries received

Returning to the works of Yaśovarman, we should note the temples built on the summits of Phnom Krom and Phnom Bok. In both cases they consist of the conventional Khmer temple, namely a set of three temple-shrines, of which the central one predominates. These two hilltop examples are built exclusively of sandstone. Those on Phnom Bok are the best preserved and in both cases the views themselves merit the climb to the summit. The Theravâdin monasteries now present interfere neither with the solitude of the ruins nor the view.

Enthusiastic for the construction of temples on imposing heights, Yaśovarman is also responsible for initiating the building of the great temple of Preah Vihear on a protruding escarpment in the Dangrek Mountains some 140 kilometres north-east of his new capital. Later monarchs up to the mid-12th century continued to embellish this impressive site with its magnificent views across the Cambodian plain to the south and the Khorat Plateau to the north. As will be noted below, from the 10th century onwards many Khmer temples were built north of the Dangrek Range, but from the 13th century onwards this whole area was gradually occupied by the encroaching Thais. Thus this range of mountains now forms the present Thai-Cambodian frontier.

When the present frontier was fixed by Franco-Thai agreement in 1907, Preah Vihear was given to Cambodia, although the escarpment on which it is built lies on the northern, Thai side of the frontier. The resulting dispute was decided at the International Court at the Hague in 1962 and it is in some ways unfortunate that the final award was made to Cambodia, since the only practicable approach is from the Thai side.[38] Khmer shrines, following the normal Indian practice, usually face east although there are several notable exceptions. Preah Vihear faces north with the main sanctuary at the far southern end of an 800-metre-long causeway that leads up through a series of five elaborate entrance portals (*gopuras*). Presumably dictated by the form of the escarpment on which it has been built,

38

32 Preah Vihear ("Holy Monastery") on a crest of the Dangrek range, founded by Yaśovarman (ruling 889 – 900), was maintained and developed by successive Angkor monarchs until the 13th century. Of these Sûryavarman I who extended Khmer hegemony ever further to the north and the west, merits special mention. Since the demise of the Khmer Empire it has been left derelict, while suffering further damage in recent times as the result of its occupation by the Khmer Rouge and subsequent fighting along the present Thai frontier. A series of five court-yards lead up to the main shine on the summit shown here, of which only broken walls remain.

33 The south side of the entrance into the third courtyard, now one of the best preserved sections of this once magnificent temple.

this temple differs radically in lay-out from other major Khmer temples, which are uniformly built within concentric enclosures on the pattern of a mandala. Further references to Preah Vihear occur below.

Yaśovarman's successor, Harshavarman, is responsible for a beautiful miniature temple-mountain, just 13 metres high, built near the foot of the hill of Bakheng, constructed of laterite and brick, impressive for its simplicity and its particularly pleasing location. It is known locally as *Baksei Chomkrong*, the "bird with spread-wings". An inscription of 947 refers to the erection in the temple of a gilded image of Śiva. Another temple, beautiful for its simplicity, built by the same king, is that known as *Kravanh* (Cardamom). It consists of a set of five linked temples, in this case constructed of brick, the centre one of which is decorated on its facing and side walls with images of Vishnu in incised brickwork. The one to the far right as seen from the front preserves a similar image of the goddess Lakshmi with kneeling figures beneath her. This temple, which looks as though newly built, is another fine example of French restoration work (1962-6).

During the reign of Harshavarman's brother, his successor, an uncle usurped the throne, taking the name of Jayavarman IV and establishing a new capital at Koh Ker, some 80 kilometres north-east of Angkor towards the Dangrek Mountains. Here he built a massive five-tier pyramid to a height of 35 metres, on which was set the Royal *linga* (presumably a newly consecrated one), named the "Lord of the Threefold World". His artists also introduced a new vigorous type of decorative sculpture, of which a fine example is that of the fight between the monkey-brothers, Sugrîva and Vâlin, to determine who should be king. The sculpture is now preserved in the Phnom Penh Museum.[39]

Jayavarman IV interested himself in further extensions to Preah Vihear, and he appears to have extended his influence well to the north of the Dangrek Range. The earliest known temples in this area are Prâsâd Khao Noi, close to the present Thai-Cambodian frontier in Aranyaprathet Province, and Prâsâd Phum Phon, far to the east of the range in the vicinity of Preah Vihear, both dating to the mid-7th century and thus contemporary with Sambor Prei Kuk, which they resemble in their brick-built style and the decoration of the lintels. The earliest temples on the Khorat Plateau (within easy reach of the modern city of Nakhon Ratchasima *alias* Khorat) are Prâsâd Non Ku and Prâsâd Muang Khaek, to the west of Khorat. They do not seem to have aroused the interest of later Khmer monarchs, but Phnom Wan, just to the north, had a long interesting history from the late 9th until at least the end of the 11th century. An inscription of 891 names Indravarman I (up to 889) who reigned at Hariharâlaya and his successor Yaśovarman (889-910) who transferred the capital to Angkor.[40] Likewise Phnom Rung, some 140 kilometres by road to the south-east of Khorat, remained an important Khmer stronghold from its foundation in the early 10th century until well into the 11th and 12th centuries (see below). This area was presumably already a small Khmer state or petty-kingdom contemporary with Jayavarman II's foundation of his capital city at Hariharâlaya (Ruluos) at

40

34 *Prâsâd Non Ku, a 7ᵗʰ century Khmer temple on the Khorat plateau (in Sung Noem District of Nakhon Ratchasima), interesting as it was constructed largely of brick like the neighbouring temple of Prâsâd Muang Khaek, and also as serving to indicate the spread of Khmer civilization northwards well beyond the Dongdek Range in this early period.*

the very beginning of the 9th century. There would appear to be still earlier associations with Îśânapura (Sambor Prei Kuk) in the 7th century, and the suzerainty of Angkor was probably acknowledged from the very foundation of this capital city. Both Phnom Rung and later Prâsâd Phimai were associated with the local ruling family, the Mahîdharapura line, which occupied the throne at Angkor on some three occasions (see below).

The death of Jayavarman IV's son, who reigned only briefly, brought to the throne King Râjendravarman (944-968), a nephew of both Yaśovarman and Jayavarman IV. He was also prince of Bhavapura, a kingdom that goes back to the time of the final defeat of Funan (see above), but later nominally accepted the suzerainty of Angkor, of which he now took possession, thus putting an end to the short-lived capital of Koh Ker.[41] Râjendravarman constructed

35 The temple-mountain, known as the East Mebon, which was built by King Râjendravarman (944-968) in the middle of the Yaśodharatatâta (the Eastern Baray) now quite dry, in honour of his parents.

two temple-mountains, one on a small island in the middle of the artificial lake built by Yaśovarman some fifty years earlier, the Yaśodharatatâka. This is referred to in guidebooks nowadays as the Eastern Baray, although there is no longer water in this vast expanse, only paddy-fields in the wet season.

This elegant temple-mountain, known popularly as the "East Mebon" to distinguish it from the "West Mebon", built a century later, now stands high and dry. Once again it has the pattern of a mandala; it is open to the four quarters with a central temple raised on a platform above the

36 Towards the end of the reign of Râjendravarman (944-968) a Brahman of high standing, related to the royal family, was responsible for the construction of the beautiful temple known popularly as "Bantay Srei" (the "Mansion for Ladies"), presumably with reference to the many images of celestial maidens (apsara) inset into the walls. It is dedicated to Tribhuvanamaheśvara, "Lord of the Threefold World". The charm of the whole temple consists in its miniature size, the rose-coloured sandstone out of which the whole complex is constructed, the elaborately worked tiered roofs of the main shrines, and the finely worked floral decoration.

43 The torana *surmounting the lintel on the western end of the northern "library" at Bantay Srei. The scene which portrays Krishna killing his wicked uncle Kamsha is especially remarkable for its portrayal of a palace, built of wood, thus giving some ideal of the many buildings of less substantial materials which once surrounded the now surviving ones of brick and stone.*

37 *The torana surmounting the lintel on the western end of the northern "library" at Bantay Srei. The scene which portrays Krishna killing his wicked uncle Kamsha is especially remarkable for its portrayal of a palace, built of wood, thus giving some ideal of the many buildings of less substantial materials which once surrounded the now surviving ones of brick and stone.*

four surrounding temples on the summit terrace. This in turn is raised on two lower square terraces, on the corners of which stand stone elephants. Eight subsidiary shrines, constructed of brick, as are also the main five temples on the summit, are arranged around the inner enclosure, two to each of the four directions. A new feature perhaps is the covered gallery which goes around the inner enclo-

38 The torana *on the western face of the eastern entrance depicts* Durgâ *in her manifestation of* Mahîshâsuramardini *("Destroyer of the Buffalo-Demon"). The buffalo, tossed upside down, is on her left, while her lion-mount rests by her right foot. There are several references to this fearful divinity in the text. See the Index.*

sure, built of laterite like the rest of the main structure. The summit temple contained the Royal *linga*, *Râjendresvara*, presumably once again a newly consecrated *linga*, identified with the king himself, while among other divinities once present were Śiva and Parvatî, who represented his own divinized parents.

His other temple-mountain, known as "Pre Rup", is some three kilometres due south of "East Mebon", near the banks of the now non-existent Eastern Baray. Although more massive, it resembles so closely its predecessor that a description is scarcely required. It consists of a triple square terrace with the now normal set of five temples on the summit. However, one notes that the upper terraces are deliberately set back towards the western side of the enclosure in order to give greater prominence to the eastern side. Moreover, an unusual feature is the row of tower-like shrines erected immediately inside the outer enclosure on the east side, intended as three to each side of the eastern entrance, although one was never finished. They are seemingly a useless addition as they spoil the symmetry of the whole design. On this occasion the Royal *linga* was known as *Râjendrabhadreśvara* ("Noble Lord King Indra") and the whole temple was dedicated to the king himself as Śiva, as well as to a favoured ancestor, identified as Vishnu, also to his maternal aunt identified as Umâ (spouse of Śiva) and to his half-brother Harshavarman, once again as Śiva.

Towards the end of Râjendravarman's reign, a Brahman of high standing, related to the royal family, constructed the beautiful temple known popularly as "Bantay Srei" (the "Mansion for Ladies"), presumably with reference to the many images of celestial maidens (*apsara*) inset into the walls. It is dedicated to *Tribhuvanamaheśvara*, "Lord of the Threefold World". The central enclosure is set within a spacious square courtyard, approached by an "avenue", now void except for fallen boundary-stones. It is from here that one enjoys the finest view of the whole complex set against the trees of the surrounding forest. The general design is conventional in that it consists of three principal shrines on a raised terrace, enclosed in a square inner enclosure, while to the left and the right as one enters this enclosure are two subsidiary buildings, conventionally referred to as "libraries". However, in front of the central shrine which is minute, there is a form of antechamber as often seen in Indian temples, and this creates perhaps an impression of overcrowding. The charm of the whole temple consists in its miniature size, the rose-coloured sandstone out of which the whole complex is constructed, the elaborately worked tiered roofs of the main shrines, and the finely worked floral decoration, which covers the walls, thus framing the deeply incised figures of

45

celestial maidens (*apsara*) and guardians. The lintels and frontal pieces (*torana*), all depicting Indian mythological scenes, are exceptionally fine. One may note especially that of Râvana, the evil king of Lanka, attempting vainly to overthrow the sacred Mountain Kailâsa, on which Śiva and Parvatî repose unconcerned, or another of Kâma, the god of love, in the act of shooting an arrow at Śiva, in order to disturb his meditation, while Parvatî stands by, rosary in hand, or again of the two monkey-brothers, Sugrîva and Vâlin, or of the goddess Mahîshâsuramardini, the "Destroyer of the Buffalo-Demon". Perhaps specially noteworthy is that of Krishna killing his wicked uncle Kamsha, depicted in a palace built of wood, thus giving some idea of the many buildings of less substantial materials which once surrounded the surviving ones of brick or stone

Although Bantay Srei in itself is exceptional, there was nothing exceptional in the foundation of temples and shrines by the high Brahmans of the court. Referring back to the Sdok Kak Thom inscription (see above), one notes that all the great prelates from Śivakaivalya in the 9th century to Sadâśiva in the 11th are credited with just such foundations. Two later inscriptions illustrate their continuance into the 12th century, as well the quantities of honours and gifts which were bestowed upon their chosen Brahman priests by Khmer monarchs.[42] If the reader is surprised at the absence of mention so far of any Buddhist foundation, it is because this powerful Brahmanical "aristocracy", often related to members of the ruling family, had at their disposal seemingly unlimited means for the founding of sanctuaries, most of which have by now disappeared, leaving only inscriptions to attest to their earlier existence. A few inscriptions may bear witness to the existence of small Buddhist communities here and there, founded by local rulers who were willing to sponsor them, and we have already noted above that Yaśovarman seemingly included them on the occasion of founding monasteries for Śaivite and Vishnuite communities on the banks of the *Yaśodharatatâka*.

CHAPTER 4
BUDDHISM IN THE 10TH AND 11TH CENTURIES

Not until the reign of Râjendravarman (944-68) is a Buddhist temple, now still standing, built within the confines of Angkor, only a few years before the construction of Bantay Srei. The promoter of this was a certain Buddhist scholar named *Kavîndrârimathana* (translatable as "Lordly Poet, Subduer of Opponents"), who was employed by the king for the construction of the East Mebon temple as well as for a palace, thus presumably winning the king's approbation and consent for the temple of Bat Chum. This

39 The modest temple of Bat Chum consisting of the basic form of three shrines, the central one higher than the other two. Built during the reign of Râjendravarman (944-968) thanks to the quite exceptional favour which a particular Buddhist prelate won at court, this is the only Buddhist temple known to have been built within the confines of Angkor before the reign of Jayavarman VII two centuries later. Revealing inscriptions concerning the condition of Buddhism in this period are carved inside the three doorways. A full account is given in the text.

modest building consists of a row of three brick-built shrines of the typical Khmer pattern with brick tiered roofs, much overgrown with lichen. Signs of decorative motifs are still visible on the centre one, which is slightly higher than the other two. They stand on a low laterite platform ascended by a flight of steps, protected by two pairs of stone lions. The site is easily reached along a small road between paddy-fields, which leads off to the right from the "Outer Circuit" between Kravanh and Sra Srang. Inscriptions on the doorways of the three towers tell us that they contained respectively images of Buddha, flanked by Vajrapâni and Prajñâpâramitâ ("Goddess Perfection of Wisdom"). They also provide information about this learned Buddhist who won the king's favour, as well as surprising information concerning the purpose of this Buddhist foundation.[41]

The three inscriptions in elegant Sanskrit verse–there is also one in Khmer–contain the same subject matter with slight variations as written by three Buddhist scholars, known as Śri Indrapandita (author of inscription A as now edited in the article referred to below), Vâp Râmabhagavat (B) and Śivacyuta- (name incomplete; C). As these texts help to reveal the relationship of Buddhism to Śaivism, as the generally established religion of the Angkor monarchs, it seems worth while to quote them at some length.

Text A opens with brief invocations to the Buddha, Lokeśvara and Vajrapâni, while B and C open with equally brief invocations to the Buddha, Vajrapâni and Prajñâpâramitâ (Goddess Perfection of Wisdom), whose images, as we learn later in all three inscriptions, reposed in the three shrines. These invocations are followed in all cases by long exaggerated praises of the reigning monarch Râjendravarman, but also providing some factual information:

Just as Kusha (son of Râma and Sîta) has done for Ayodhyâ, he restored the holy city of Yaśodharapurî which had remained empty for a long time, rendering it magnificent and beautiful with buildings of brilliant gold and palaces of gems like the palace of great Indra on earth. In the centre of the ocean, the sacred lake of Yaśodhara, he erected images of Brahmâ, Śiva and Vishnu as well as a linga (A: vv.13-14, B: v.20 and C: v.25).

The praises of the ruling monarch (*sine qua non*) are followed by those of Kavîndrârimathana himself, although only text C specifies that he was personally responsible for the various works mentioned above:

With no other concern apart from the Buddhist doctrine and although foremost amongst fellow-Buddhists, he was attached in his devotion to his king, the "Supreme Lord" (Parameśvara = Śiva). Beloved of this Lord of Men, an Architect like Viśvakarman, he was entrusted by the King to build a beautiful palace in Yaśodharapura, and by general approbation he was enjoined to create (an island of) rock and other constructions in the middle of the Yaśodhara Lake (C: vv.33-35).

Text B adds rather more specific details concerning his Buddhist benefactions, especially at Bat Chum itself:

Having united the identity of his own self with the divine self-nature of the Buddha, he acquired Yogic Knowledge (yogijñāna) as inherent within his own mind. Triumphantly he erected at Jayantadeśa an image of the Buddha and at Kutîśvara a Buddha-image flanked by two goddesses. Having erected these several shines he offered them as temples for the divinity to dwell there, just as in the lotus of his own heart.

Furthermore this ordinance of which the King in his divine palace is informed, must be carried out by wise and good men. These posses-sions dedicated to the gods will not be taken by honest people, and may our rulers seize evil men intent on theft! If a single tree which provides shade is not to be cut here, how much less should one cut the timbers which provide contentment for those who seek bliss. Here there dwell monks intent only upon a moral life, their minds preoccu-pied with the good of others, peaceful in their meditation (C: vv. 30-37).

The rather surprising verses which follow and bring the inscription to an end are more or less the same in all three inscriptions:

A: v.21: With the exception of the sacrificial priest (hotar), the high-est among Brahmans, no one may bathe here in this water which comes from a bathing-place on the summit of the holy mountain of Śrî Mahendragiri (Phnom Kulen), in this sanctified water of this holy pool, which procures great merit although there is little of it.

B: v.38: With the exception of a Brahman who knows the Veda no one may bathe in the pure water of this great pool which has been dug ritually.

C: vv.38-41: (Kavîndrârimathana) has constructed this pool, which purifies with its pure water just as knowledge leads to nirvâna. In

*accordance with Buddhist ritual he has created this pool, honoured
by the great and intended to bring joy to living beings, while contrib-
uting to the prosperity of the Dharma. In the sacred water of this
lake, worthy of the frolics of flamingos, only the King's chief prelate
(purohita) and Brahmans have the right to bathe. Elephants which
destroy the banks of this pool must be kept away by the lion-like
sâdhus (holy men) with the hair-style of the Dharma (presumably
meaning the shaven-headed monks who live in this monastery).*

Text A ends with a further warning against those who
might rob this place. It would seem that the inscriptions
are primarily concerned with the dedication of the pool,
which can only be used by Brahmans, and of which this
small community of Buddhist monks were the appointed
keepers. Other inferences will be noted below with reference to another such inscription.

Râjendravarman's reign was followed by that of
Jayavarman V (968-1001). During his reign work was begun on two major projects, that of building yet another
temple-mountain (Ta Keo) and of building or possibly re-
constructing the temple in the palace grounds, known correctly as Phimean-akas, being the regular Khmer pronunciation of Sanskrit *Vimâna-akâśa*, meaning "Aerial Palace". The palace grounds measure 250 by 600 metres, and
the only building still standing is this "Aerial Palace". It
consists of a series of three steeply rising square terraces on
which stood originally the regular group of five shrines,
built of laterite and sandstone. Of these very little remain,
but much of the surrounding covered gallery, such as we
noted before on the East Mebon, still remains. The view is
magnificent and especially interesting towards the
Baphuon (see below) which is immediately to the south.

Viewed directly from the front (east side), I find Ta Keo
remarkably similar in appearance to the "Aerial Palace".
It rises up as a steep five-terraced pyramid of laterite, surmounted by the usual five summit shrines, in this case built
of sandstone and rather box-like in their present forlorn
condition. One notes that all these five summit shrines
are open to the four directions, and that each shrine has
attached antechambers to each of its four sides. In the case

40 The Phimean-akas, or "Aerial Palace", the only building which still stands within the palace grounds, a vast walled rectangle of 600 by 250 metres. It was in effect the palace temple, constructed like other temple-mountains mainly of laterite, while the royal quarters and subsidiary buildings would all have been of more fragile materials. Lying some two kilometres due north of the Bakheng, which was established as centre of his new city by Yaśovarman about the year 900, this site quite possibly served as the royal quarters since about the same time. The "Aerial Palace" as one sees it today dates from the end of the 10th century and the beginning of the 11th, having been constructed during the reigns of Jayavarman V (968-1001) and Sûryavarman I (soon after 1001 to 1050). It consists of a steeply rising pyramid, 38 by 28 metres at the base and 30 by 23 on the summit platform.

of the central shrine, as usual appreciably larger than the others, these antechambers have a double structure. It is impressive, but perhaps massively ugly in its present denuded condition. Neither of these great works was finished during Jayavarman V's reign because of disputes regarding the succession and consequent internal wars.

This monarch also looked with favour upon a certain Buddhist prelate named Kîrtipandita, who appears to have served him at court and was responsible for numerous Buddhist foundations. The evidence for this derives from a stone inscription at Vat Sithor in the province of Kampong Cham.[44] After praises of the Buddha, manifest in his Self-Existent Body (*dharmakâya*), his Glorious Body (*sambhogakâya*) and his Transformation Body (*nirmânakâya*), followed by that of the Doctrine (*Dharma*) and of the Community (*Sangha*), conceived in Mahâyâna terms as the assembly of Bodhisattvas and their disciples, there follows the usual eulogy of the reigning monarch (Jayavarman V), where the date of Śaka 890 (AD 968) is given as the commencement of his reign. One may note that in verse 49 of the inscription the earlier date of Śaka 869 (AD 947) is given as referring to Kîrtipandita's major foundation at a placename of which the first syllable is missing. This doubtless refers to Vat Sithor itself, which this great Buddhist prelate must have founded during the reign of the previous king Râjendravarman. Of primary interest however is the account of Kîrtipandita's person and of his manifold activities.

Verse 27 onwards: In him the sun of the doctrines of "Non-Self" (nairâtmya), "Mind Only" (çittamâtra) and the like, which have been eclipsed in the night of false teachings, shone once again in full daylight.

On the path of the Holy Dharma he relit the torch of the "Discourse on discrimination between the middle and the extremes" (Madyântavibhâga) and other treatises which had been extinguished by evil winds.

Having sought for a host of philosophical books and treatises, such as the commentary on the "Compendium of Truth" (Tattvasamgraha), this sage spread wide their study.[45]

Verse 36 onwards: Loaded with honours by the king on account of his zeal for the protection of the circle of the realm, he was responsible for the performance within the palace of the rites of pacification, prosperity and so on.[46] In order to save fellow-Buddhists from misfortune, he re-established the image of the Muni (Teacher, viz. Lord Buddha) fashioned with devotion, of which the throne had been broken. He provided joyously an entry-portal, enriched with gold and silver for the image of the Muni.

In order to gain for himself as well as for others the supreme and incomparable Way of salvation, he offered the Lord Buddha two royal palanquins of gold and of silver. As residence for the Lord he dedicated a large shrine with a tiered roof of copper, adorned with gold and precious stones as well as a lion-throne. In order to gain the fruits of merit for others in the excellent field of merit, he dedicated to the Lord paddy-fields producing 4,000 khâri (an uncertain measure of weight).

Having established the doctrine in its normal and its hidden form, he erected ashrams for the cult both for monks and for religious laymen. He offered to the Buddha male and female elephants, horses, buffaloes and cows in great number, as well as ashrams, treasures and slaves, male and female.

He erected in this place for the illumination of the lineage of the Omniscient One an image of the all-saving Perfection of Wisdom, the Mother of all-saving Buddhas. He erected more than ten images of Vajrapâni (Vajrin) and Avalokiteśvara (Lokeśa), which had been previously consecrated on a hill-top by Śri Satyavarman, and whose thrones were broken. On a high summit in the town of Kurârambha, also at Amarendrapura and other places, he set up images of Avalokiteśvara and so on. Having restored in great numbers in various places the images of the Buddha which had been broken, he set them up anew and installed pools and ashrams. In the year Śaka 869 (AD 947) this teacher of men, accompanied by his disciples, founded on his own initiative shrines with innumerable images of the Lord in the village of (?Dha)rmapattana for his own benfit and that of others (vv. 36-49).

As for the regulation of monastic life, it was ordained that a monthly festival be held in accordance with the twelve "lunar mansions" (*nakshatra*).

Verse 56 onwards: Also in accordance with an ancient order of the Great Muni the monastery gong, placed to the south-east side of the complex, should be sounded thrice daily. Those who are attentive, even by mental reflection, to its sound, which has a purifying effect in that it announces the times for monastic ceremonies, these are the happy ones who make their way towards heaven. May he gain great merit, who thus founds a monastery (vihâra) for the good of others, offering it to the Three Precious Ones!

All the bounty intended for the Three Precious Ones should be assigned separately in three parts, and not all mixed together. (Presumably this means one part for the Buddha [viz. the cult of the images], one part for the Doctrine [viz. for study and copying of manuscripts] and one part for the Community [viz. the monks themselves]).

Unless a monastery has been properly consecrated by the monks, it is no monastery, but just a treasury (kosthâgara). Such a foundation is made for material interests, but not for the benefit of others and for the sake of religious calm. In such a place there is no pure merit where omniscience can be obtained. Where a monastery has been founded according to the proper rule, the merit spreads everywhere at once just like space itself.

May those evil men who destroy such merit, experience endlessly the sufferings of hell! The layfolk shall not use for their own profit the property of the monastery. This would be poison for them. Spells may cure (normal) poison, but not that deriving from (the misappropriation of) monastic property.

Having completed with devotion this command of the Omniscient Lord, viz. the founding of this monastery in accordance with the rule, the self-controlled ones (monks) settled there permanently. The virtuous, the peaceful and the learned are superior to ordinary folk, and whoever desires merit, assigns various goods for their benefit.

At dawn and at other proper hours the ceremonies, as ordained by the Lord for the self-controlled (monks), should be performed by the community and especially by the chief officiant. Unless specially assigned, the Buddhist community should not attend (Brahmanical) sacrificial ceremonies. Those who go on their own account, even with good intentions, are guilty of an offence.

The prelate (purohita) who is expert in the homa rites with their secret hand-gestures (mudra), mantras and spells, and who knows the secret of Vajra and Bell, is worthy of his fees (vv.56-69).

From this and the previous quotation from the inscription of Bat Chum one can deduce a few ideas concerning the state of Buddhism in the Khmer empire of the10th and 11th centuries. Just like the numerous Brahmanical foundations, it depended upon the munificence of wealthy prelates who had won the monarch's or some local ruler's favour. But Buddhism was clearly at a disadvantage, especially within the confines of the capital city of Angkor. As explained above, the lineages of influential Brahmans, often related to the leading aristocratic families, formed an essential part of the structure of the state at least from the time of Jayavarman II onwards. I have already referred above to the numerous Brahmanical foundations sponsored by royal favour as a continuous process from one reign to the next, such as are recorded on the Sdok Kak Thom stele. By contrast only an occasional Buddhist prelate of note seems to have won the king's favour and in both cases noted here, it would have appear to have been due to architectural and building skills and with no direct relevance to religion.

One notes that Kîrtipandita was also invited to perform small auspicious ceremonies within the palace, but such ceremonies were certainly already being performed by the king's Brahmanical entourage, and one may well imagine that the Brahmans regarded such a Buddhist intrusion as unnecessary. Only the king's command would have made this possible. One certainly has the impression that Buddhism remains on the defensive, formally acknowledging that Brahmanical cults represent the state religion. This is expressed clearly enough when it is written of Kavindrârimathana that "with no other concern apart from the Buddhist doctrine and although foremost amongst Buddhists, he was attached in his devotion to the King, the Supreme Lord (*Parameśvara* = Śiva)". Not only were images of the great Hindu gods often set up at Buddhist shrines, but in the case of Bat Chum the sacred pool was primarily reserved for the use of Brahmanical prelates. This certainly does not represent an amalgamation of Hinduism and Buddhism, such as developed in eastern Java, where kings were formally identified with the great Mahâyâna and tantric Buddhist divinities, and where Buddhist prelates of the highest rank (*vajrâçârya*) eventually assume the same rank as Brahmans, a situation which still exists in a popularized form in Nepal and in Bali.

It seems clear from these two inscriptions that Buddhism persisted in Cambodia as a religion essentially separate and doctrinally hostile to Brahmanical religion, although it would have been politically disastrous to express such hostility overtly. Monastic life continued probably in accordance with the Vinaya (monastic discipline) of the *Mûlasarvâstivâdins*, which was the form mainly followed throughout South-East Asia, as is testified by I-tsing.[47]

I wonder what the author of the inscription has in mind when he states that a monastery that has not been properly consecrated is no more than a "treasury" *(kosthâgara)*. Such is the primary meaning of the Sanskrit term, although it may also mean a storeroom or godown. It may refer to privately endowed Buddhist shrines cared for by one or two monks or religious laymen, and if so this suggests the existence of a more general Buddhist following in the country. Owing to the total lack of any surviving literature, Buddhist or otherwise, apart from the stone inscriptions (very different from the situation in East Java), it is impossible to gain any clear ideas on this subject. We may also note that Kîrtipandita "established the Holy Doctrine in its usual and its secret form", which refers to regular monastic establishments as well as the performance of tantric ritual for the gaining of enlightenment in a single lifetime. Within this same context we may note the reference to "the priest who is expert in the *homa* rites with their secret hand-gestures, mantras and spells and who knows the secret of Vajra and Bell."

The same situation was typical of Tibet in precisely the same period, thus reproducing the forms which Mahâyâna Buddhism had already assumed in northern India. Whereas much is known concerning the part that tantric Buddhism played in Tibet, practically nothing is known of the scope of tantric Buddhism in Cambodia, simply because of the total absence of the relevant literature. (See further on this subject below.)

The range of Mahâyâna divinities, of whom the most popular are Avalokiteśvara (Lokeśa), Vajrapâni (Vajrin) and Prajñâ, is very limited indeed compared with northern India and Tibet and even with Java. Buddhism can scarcely have held much sway throughout the Khmer Empire except in the north-west, where Buddhism was already well established thanks to the Mon populations to the north of the Gulf of Siam. However, the rapidity with

41 A particularly fine life-size of Avalokiteśvara on the west side of Neak Poen. This small shrine, constructed by order of Jayavarman VII in the centre of its own moat and in the middle of the Jayatatâka, "Lake of Victory", is dedicated to Avalokiteśvara, while representing the quasi-mythical Anavatapta Lake in the Himalayas. An identical image on the east side has recently been the victim of these continuing wicked thefts, the whole face having been cut away for the benefit of some trafficker in "works of art".

42 Judging by the number of images of Hevajra found around Angkor and on various sites on the Khorat Plateau in Thailand, as witnessed by the several examples which can be seen on the Bangkok Museum, it would seem that a cult of this important tantric divinity was practised from the 11th century onwards. Since no relevant literature is available, not even a stray reference on a carved inscription, nothing of certainty can be said regarding this cult. From the iconography I note that Hevajra appears as a single male divinity, while in Indian and Tibetan represen-tation, he is more usually coupled with his feminine partner Nairâtmyâ. (With acknowledgement to the Bangkok Museum for this illustration.)

57

43 A later form of Avalokiteśvara, 12th century onwards, of which there are many examples, shows him in an eight-armed manifestation with the upper torso, covered as it were in a close-fitting tunic of armour, actually consisting of miniature Buddha-images, which he radiates through the eight directions of space. (With acknowledgement to the Bangkok Museum.)

which Theravâdin Buddhism spread once the central royal authority was weakened (13th century onwards) suggests that the general population, overtaxed by the seemingly never-ending construction of so many Brahmanical monuments, may well have been more open to the ministrations of the small Buddhist communities who probably existed in their midst. As for the practical religious interests of simple people generally, these surely related to ancestor cults and the placating of local spirits, which is still the case today.

44 *The stone torso of a standing bejewelled Buddha-image, making the hand gesture of fearlessnesss (abhaya), suggesting protection to his devotees. Of unknown origin, it now reposes in the British Museum, where acknowledgements are due for this illustration.*

45 In his supreme manifestation the Buddha is usually represented in the later period as seated in mediation under the protection of the nâga Muçalinda. This particular manifestation relates to the story of Śâkyamuni's final stage of meditation leading to his enlightenment, when this nâga approached him respectfully, wrapped him in his coils, while extending his hood over the sacred head, in order to protect him from the elements. Although well known in all other Buddhist traditions, only in Cambodia is this particular manifestation envisaged as representing the supreme manifestation of buddhahood. (With acknowledgement to the Bangkok Museum.)

At the same time there probably existed in official circles, wherever Brahmanical cults prevailed, an antagonism to Buddhism. There is also much mention in the last inscription of the need to repair broken Buddhist shrines, which suggests either poor maintenance or even deliberate destruction by ill-wishers, who are also specifically mentioned. This last appears to be a continual preoccupation of the founders of Buddhist sanctuaries.[48] Such antagonism to Buddhism would not be surprising within the context of strong Brahmanical hold on the political centre of power. The evidence for this certainly exists in the case of Buddhist monuments of Jayavarman VII, as will be related below, and thus it would not be surprising if the same hostility were shown during the previous centuries. The very rarity of Buddhist monuments within the wide limits of the capital city of Angkor before Jayavarman VII assumed power is enough in itself to suggest the low esteem in which Buddhism was held in the official royal Brahmanical circles.

CHAPTER 5
THE KHMER EMPIRE

The Khmer Empire (suitably called such from the 11th century onwards) remained a single authoritarian power only for limited periods, whenever there was a powerful military ruler on the throne; there was no stabilised order of succession. The earlier capitals of Wat Phu, Bhavapura, Îśânapura (Sambor Prei Kuk) and others in the south going back to the time of Lower Chenla in the 8th century, not even then a unified state, remained centres of local power with local "kings" (*kurun*), most of whom could claim relationship in one royal family or another. In case of weakness at the centre in Angkor, any one of these could make a claim on the throne.[49] Such was the case of the next great king of note, namely Sûryavarman I. He seems

46 View towards Battambang, some 20 kms distant, from Phnom Banon, the hilltop, about 80 metres high, on which stands a group of five shrines. This 11th century foundation, apart from its impressive position, is remarkable as being originally a Buddhist foundation. Two of its toranas show Śâkyamuni on a lotus-throne.

to have come from Śambupura (Sambor), known from the
8th century as one of the states of Lower Chenla, or he
may have first occupied Sambor in 1001, then Îśânapura
the following year, whence he made his attack on Angkor,
defeating two other claimants to the throne. He claimed
family connections with both Indravarman and
Yaśovarman, thus going back to the 9th century. All the

*47 A third torana on the south side of the eastern tower of Phnom
Banon shows a ten-armed tantric divinity, similar to the one seen at
Phimai (near Khorat), whom I have identified tentatively as
Trailokyavijaya (see below).*

great Khmer kings received posthumous names relating
them to the divinity with whom they had chosen to identify themselves. I have avoided quoting these, as the text
is already heavy with too many names, but in the case of
Sûryavarman, his posthumous name of Nirvânapada should
be mentioned, as possibly indicative of his personal Buddhist proclivities. One notes at the same time that he came
from the south of the country, where Buddhism was probably better fostered than at the court of Angkor. This did
not prevent him conforming to the already established
order and he took as his prelate the Brahman Sadâśiva,
who had only recently served under one of the defeated
rivals. He became a favourite of the king, who released
him from his vow of celibacy (and inevitably his duties as
"high-priest" of the "Royal linga" rite), so as to arrange his
marriage with the sister of the king's own wife. Sadâśiva
thus received new titles and also the new name of Śrî
Jayendrapandita. He immediately set about repairing the
damage of the recent warfare relating to the succession.

63

48 Vat Ek, some 8 kms north of Battambang. Founded in 1027,
Śaivite, in a beautiful situation beside a lotus-lake and a Theravâdin
monastery of the same name.

49 Vat Ek contains some unusual toranas, such as this one (on the south side) of Śiva dancing between two prancing horses a garlanded design.

50 A small shrine by the wayside at the village of Steung, some 20 kms south-west of Battambang along the road to Pailin. It once formed part of a larger complex, of which three towers, about 200 metres distant, were part. It is simply known as Prâsâd Steung, a name which also applies to the Theravâdin monastery on the same site. This small shrine is remarkable for its unusual lintels.

As for the sites of Bhadrapattana and the sites of Stuk Ransi and all their establishments, completely devastated when His Majesty advanced with his forces, the Lord Śri Jayendrapandita completely rebuilt these sites and reconsecrated the images which had been set up there. At the Bhadrapattana site he set up a linga and two more images other than those belonging to the family-line. He gave all the items necessaries for these sanctuaries, he gave slaves, he built a "watch-tower" (valabhi), he built an enclosure of laterite, he made fields and gardens, he dug a reservoir and made a dike.[50] *At the Bhadrâvasa site he consecrated the images of the gods, he reordered*

65

51 *A scene of Churning the Ocean, presided over by Vishnu, with Brahma above in the company of gods, Prâsâd Steung.*

52 *Another such lintel showing a row of gods or sages, supported by demonic figures.*

the site, he made a dike, an enclosure, a cattle-pen and all the sacred
cows for this sanctuary. At the Ransi site, he consecrated the statues,
gave the necessary items, dug a pool, made a park, dug a reservoir
and made a dike.

Apart from such repair works, the East Mebon and Ta
Keo temples were completed, as well as entrance porticoes
for the palace grounds. He also built or added to temples
throughout the realm, such as Phnom Chisor in the far
south near the ancient sites of Ta Keo and Angkor Borei,
as well as temples in the vicinity of Battambang. The most
impressive of these, with a magnificent view of the surrounding plain, is a typical group of five shrines built on
the summit of a hill, 80 metres high, known as Phnom
Banon, some 20 kilometres south of Battambang.

Of greater archaeological importance is Prâsâd Baset,
some 12 kilometres east of the city, seemingly founded
during the last years of the reign of Sûryavarman I. The
central shrine, with its extended antechamber, was set
within three rectangular courtyards, the outer being about
200 metres square and the inner one about 50. It was approached by a series of three *gopuras* on the east and west
sides, with subsidiary towers to the north and south of the
main shrine. Once covered with fine sculptures, this site is
now a total ruin.

66

Vat Ek, about eight kilometres north of Battambang,
merits a visit for the tranquillity and beauty of its setting
beside a lotus-covered lake and the very much later
Theravâdin monastery of the same name. It consists now
of little more than the main shrine with its regular antechamber within a walled enclosure of about 50 metres
square, entered by *gopuras* on the east (front) and west
sides. It retains some good lintels of Śiva and Parvatî on
Nandin, of a dancing Śiva and of the scene of the Churning of the Ocean. It was founded by a Brahman prelate
named Yogîśvara Pandita in 1027 AD.[51] A very small temple by the roadside in the village of Steung, about 20 kilometres south-west of Battambang, is remarkable simply for
well preserved lintels of Vishnu reposing while giving birth
to Brahma on a lotus-stalk from his navel, a miniature scene

of "Churning the Ocean", with rishis above, one of the Pândava brothers playing dice with their Kaurava contestants, and one of a row of sages supported by demonic figures. About 200 metres from the road one comes upon a row of three typical Khmer brick-built shrines standing solitarily near the more recent Theravâdin monastery.

Sûryavarman I further embellished Preah Vihear in the far north, the building initiated by Yaśovarman (see above). Further work had been done there by Râjendravarman II and Jayavarman V during the 10th century. Sûryavarman now added to the buildings in the outer court and built avenues lined with ornamental balustrades. However, he was more famous as a successful warrior than a builder of temples. He expanded the boundary of Khmer interests westwards across the Khorat Plateau, and thus into the Chao Phraya Valley and the whole area around the Gulf of Siam, and thence south down the Malay Peninsula at least as far as Phetchaburi.

Lopburi (then known as Lavo) to the north became a Khmer regional capital. The earliest Khmer temple, known locally as Prang Khaek, dating back to the end of of the 10th century, still stands with its three brick towers in the middle of a traffic island. More impressive temples were built later, namely Wat Mahathat in a far more spacious layout, as well as Prang Sam Yod, similar to Prang Khaek, but in a more imposing setting.[52] These last two, dating to the reign of Jayavarman VII, were Buddhist foundations, but even in this Mon region, where Buddhism flourished long before and during the Khmer occupation, there are indications that they were subsequently converted into Śaivite shrines. This could only have occurred under the direct orders of the local Khmer governor of the province, indicating once again that the established religion of state was essentially Brahmanical.

From the 11th century onwards several impressive temples, all now in Thailand, were built on the Khorat Plateau. The most notable are Phnom Rung on its impressive hilltop, the nearby Muang Tam at the foot of the same hill and Prâsâd Phimai, further to the north, the only one that

53 The Khmer temple known as Prang Khaek in Lopburi, now in
Thailand. Long before the arrival of the Thais in what is now
Thailand, Suryavarman I (1002-1050) extended Khmer
overlordship around the Gulf of Siam, an area then occupied
primarily by the Mon.

68

is overtly Buddhist, although once again Hindu motifs are
present.[53]

Although smaller in design, all these major temples are
laid out on the same general design as Angkor Vat, as built
a century later by Sûryavarman II, namely as a central towering shrine set within a series of square enclosures. For

54 The Wat Mahathat at Lopburi, which was a Khmer provincial
capital from the early 11th until the late 13th century, when as a
result of the general retreat in the fortunes of the Khmer empire,
Lopburi was able assert its independence until absorbed into the
kingdom of Ayuthaya (Siam) in the mid-14th century. Only the
central shrine with its mandapa are originally Khmer, The
surrounding shrines are later Ayuthaya (Thai) style.

temples of less august importance, a set of three shrines remains the normal Khmer pattern, as already described above with regard to the 9th-century temples at Ruluos, the Prang Khaek and Prang Sam Yod at Lopburi, mentioned just above.

The extension of Khmer influence ever further south down the Thai-Malay peninsula was bound to create conflict with the maritime empire of Śrivijâya, which included the southern part of the same peninsula at least as far north as Chaiya. Sûryavarman made friendly gestures (c.1012) to the Çola monarch of South India, Râjendraçola I, offering him the gift of a chariot, presumably anticipating conflict with Śrivijaya on the campaign to the south on which he was about to embark.[54] In the event there was no such difficulty, as Śrivijaya was soon involved in withstanding the Çola invasion of 1025. This invasion probably allowed the Khmers to extend their interests thus far down the peninsula.

69

Sûryavarman was succeeded by a nephew, Udayâdityavarman II (1050-66), who loaded the Brahman Sadâśiva with further honours and gifts, while authorizing the construction of the Śaivite shrine at Sdok Kak Thom (Badraniketana), of which a commemoration stone con-

55 The reconstructed eastern gopura of the Baphuon, the enormous temple-mountain constructed by Udayâdityavarman II in the second half of the 11th century. A long-term French programme of restoration is in progress, to be completed by the year 2005.

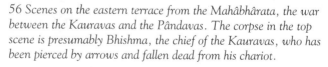

56 Scenes on the eastern terrace from the Mahâbhârata, the war
between the Kauravas and the Pândavas. The corpse in the top
scene is presumably Bhishma, the chief of the Kauravas, who has
been pierced by arrows and fallen dead from his chariot.

tains important information concerning the origin of the
Devarâja ritual (see above).[55] Already famed as the architect for Sûryavarman's construction works, it was probably
Sadâśiva who was responsible for the building of yet another temple-mountain. It followed the conventional form
of an enormous five-tiered pyramid, but with steeper sides.

57 Scenes from the Râmâyana on the eastern terraces of the Baphuon: the testing of Sita's fidelity and Râma and Sita enthroned together.

It is approached by a fine stone-built avenue 200 metres long, but regrettably the Baphuon now presents itself as a rounded mass of collapsed masonry, while substantial restoration works are continually in process. A large number of bas-reliefs have survived, some of classical scenes from the Ramâyana and the Krishna legend, and seemingly other

58 This section of carved panels, illustrating the unusual scene of the waking from slumber the rakshasa *Kumbhakarna, one of the main champions in the battle of Lanka in the* Râmâyana. *It was found buried under the body of the lying Buddha. See pp. 133-4.*

more popular scenes such as appear later on the Bayon.[56]

Udayâdityavarman's major contribution to the economic life of the country was the construction of an enormous new reservoir, an artificial lake 8 by 2.2 kilometres in size. Now known as the Western Baray, it is the only one of these great reservoirs to survive, on which the prosperity of Angkor depended. I quote from a section in D.G.E.Hall's *History of South-East Asia*, entitled "The economic basis of Khmer civilization", which helps to explain how an agricultural community could attain such power and such wealth, even though this remained in the hands of a few.

The Khmers, who had inherited methods of irrigation from Funan, found the Angkor region ideal for the purpose of constructing a system of water utilization that would cause the soil to yield its utmost in the service of man. The city itself, so far from being an urban agglomeration, was rather a collection of waterworks stretching far and wide beyond the palace and its immediate temples, with a considerable population densely settled along its causeways and canals, and much of its land cut up into cultivated holdings. In this connection modern research has established the significant fact that each Khmer king, upon taking office, was expected to carry out works 'of public interest', particularly works of irrigation. Indeed, Monsieur Groslier goes so far as to say that the labour bestowed upon the ever-developing irrigation system is 'far more impressive than the building of temples, which were merely chapels crowning a cyclopean undertaking.'

A translated quotation from Groslier's text draws attention to the symbolic relationship between the irrigation system and the popular legendary motif of the "Churning of the Ocean" in order to produce the elixir of life.

One knows the celebrated phrase of Jayavarman VII regarding the founding of Angkor Thom: 'The city of Yaśodharapurî (here given a feminine gender), clad with Jayasindhu, was taken as wife by the king for the producing of happiness for the world'. The Jayasindhu, namely the moat around Angkor Thom, is effectively "churned" by the giants on the bridges which cross it. Thus we know the rôle of the moats from the hydraulic viewpoint, and how they brought prosperity to the country by distributing the water of the barays for irrigation. What in fact is a baray and the canals which it feeds? The inscriptions inform us: 'It is a vast basin like a Sea of Milk'. What does the king actually do in constructing such works? 'By his efforts the Sea of Milk itself, freed of its water content, becomes a Sea of Nectar'. Thus in a general way the theme of the "Churning of the Ocean" represents the same "churning" by the king in order to produce the nectar which is the happiness of his subjects.[57]

Udayâdityavarman's reign was troubled by internal wars, and his successor Harshavarman III found himself at war with the Chams, who burned the city of Śambhupura (Sambor), destroying its sanctuaries and carrying off Khmers as slaves to their sanctuaries at home. His unsettled reign was followed by that of a usurper, a local ruler who fought his way to power. He was followed by his son who reigned only five years, and then, in unclear but clearly unsettled circumstances, a grand-nephew of the latter gained possession of the throne. This was Sûryavarman II (1113-1150), famous as a great warrior and as the founder of Angkor Vat, the largest and most ambitious of all these various "temple-mountains". In the east he maintained continual campaigns against Champa by land and by sea, eventually occupying the capital of Vijaya (Binh-dinh), situated more than halfway down the east coast of Indo-China. He also turned his attentions against the Vietnamese (Dai-Viêt) and their capital at Nghê-an (near modern Vinh) with no apparent success, even though he was then in league with the Chams. His wars on this front served no useful purpose and three decades later the Chams took terrible vengeance. The wars in the west appear to have started when the Mons of Haripuñjaya (a kingdom centred on Lamphun) assaulted Lavo (Lopburi), already a province of the Khmer Empire. The famous frieze on the west wing of the southern gallery of Angkor Vat shows Sûryavarman in warlike procession followed by a Syam warrior and by the ruler of Lavo, both regarded as allies in this war.[58]

During his reign several temples, quite apart from Angkor Vat, were built or underwent extensive reconstruction. Four important ones are Phnom Rung, Muang Tam and Phimai (original name Vimâya) on the Khorat Plateau, and Ta Muen Thom, built near the pass across the Dangrek Mountains on the way from Angkor to the plateau.

Phnom Rung, known with certainty from the 10th century onwards, was embellished by a local ruler, named Narendrâditya, who like Virendrâdhipativarman, was one of the major supporters of Sûryavarman II. According to an inscription set up by his son in 1150, he received local suzerainty as a result of the armed support which he had given to his sovereign. He followed Brahmanical tradition, ending his life as a Hindu ascetic, and Phnom Rung, like the majority of important Khmer temples, was dedicated to Śiva.[59]

Such an isolated hilltop, rising to 383 metres, with a superb view of the surrounding plain, would certainly have invited early interest in the site, as with Preah Vihear. The shape of the hill allows for an impressive approach from the east, along an "avenue" marked by small lotus-topped boundary posts for a distance of 160 metres. Thence a wide terrace with *nâga*-balustrades leads into the impressive east-

59 Phnom Rung, built on the summit of a small extinct volcano some 95 kms south-east of Nakhon Ratchasima (Khorat) was another important Khmer local capital, dating from the early 10th until the late 12th century. Here it is seen from the main eastern gopura.

60 As Phnom Rung was built on a hilltop with very limited space around, it seems to have been closely associated with another important Khmer temple at the very foot of the same hill. This is Muang Tam, which has been recently most beautifully restored. Unfortunately so little remained of the main central shrine, set within a group of four others, that its reconstruction proved impossible. At the same time, the beauty of whole complex is greatly enhanced by the lotus-pools at the four corners.

ern *gopura*, whence one confronts at once the eastern front
of the *mandapa* (antechamber) surmounted by a figure of a
dancing Śiva, and below him the reclining figure of Vishnu.
The space on the summit allows only for a single rectangular walled enclosure, in the centre of which stands the
main shrine with the antechamber. This last contains an
image of Śiva's mount, the bull Nandin, while the main
shrine would have contained a *linga*, now absent. The frontal pieces (*torana*) over the doorways are decorated with
Hindu themes, mainly from the Râmâyana. As is usual,
the main shrine is not exactly central, being placed slightly
to the west, so as to leave space for the more elaborate
approach from the east.

Phnom Rung can never have been the centre of a "city"
like Phimai, but this function was doubtless performed by
the temple of Muang Tam at the foot of the hill, likewise
dedicated to Śiva. In the absence of inscriptions, it is usually dated to the 11th century by the style of the carvings
on its lintels.

The main charm of Muang Tam is the moat with its

61 *Muang Tam is also notable for its fine carved toranas
illustrating popular Hindu themes. Here we see Brahma enthroned
on his sacred geese* (hamsa), *surmounting the usual Kâla mask
with elaborate garlands issuing from his mouth.*

62 The central shrine of Phimai as seen from the southern gopura of the second enclosure. Formerly linked to Angkor by one of the main highways constructed throughout the empire by Jayavarman VII, it remains as one of the most important Khmer temples now in Thailand. A city in its own right, as explained in the text, it lies 60 kms to the north-west of Nakhon Ratchasima (Khorat). Founded in the 11ᵗʰ century as a provincial capital, it has the distinction of being a Buddhist foundation, when other Khmer provincial capitals tended to be Śaivite out of deference to the Brahmanical traditions of Angkor.

flowering lotuses, which lies between the inner and the outer enclosure. The moat consists of four angular segments, thus allowing approach from all four directions. The inner temple consists of a group of five brick-built towers. The centre one is regrettably absent because there were insufficient pieces remaining from the ruins for its reconstruction. However, some very fine lintels remain *in situ*, mainly repeating the same motif of a *kâla* mask clutching a *nâga*-like garland in its mouth, with a small inset theme which is variable, such as Brahma riding a triad of geese, a multi-armed Krishna defeating a demon or simply a *rishi* (ascetic) in repose.

Phimai was a major regional capital, associated in several inscriptions with the kings of the so-called Mahîdharapura Dynasty, namely Jayavarman VI, Dharanindravarman I, seemingly Sûryavarman II, and also Jayavarman VII.[60] The main temple is enclosed within a double square enclosure. Although of rather simplified dimensions, the temple-complex has the same general pattern as Angkor Vat, namely a square (slightly rectangular) courtyard, entered by portals (*gopura*) to the four directions. On the south (primary) side of the central towered sanctuary, preceded as usual by an antechamber (*mandapa*), there stand two subsidiary shrines. This central complex is approached by a beautifully restored *nâga*-railed bridge, which leads in from the main (southern) *gopura* to the second enclosure, 274 by 220 metres. This central temple complex is set with an outer rectangular enclosure (1020

78

63 *Phimai: a lintel over a doorway at the north-eastern corner of the gallery. For reasons given in the text, I would identify this divinity as Trailokyavijaya, a powerful tantric emanation of Vajrapâni.*

by 580 m.) which corresponds fairly closely with the present city limits. Phimai thus presents the rare example of an outer walled enclosure ("city limits") of a Khmer temple-complex, still filled with the dwellings, albeit rather more modern ones, of the local population. At Angkor and elsewhere we are used to seeing Khmer temple-complexes, such as Angkor Vat, set in the midst of a vast empty park, or Preah Khan and similar foundations, standing in the midst of an outer enclosure now entirely overgrown with jungle.

Here at Phimai there once dwelt the local aristocracy, the Brahmans and Buddhist monks accredited to the main shrine, the staff and retainers, all in far less durable accommodation, which has long since disappeared. Doubtless the present population of Phimai has no great concern with the magnificent temple in their midst, except as a valuable tourist attraction, but at least they fill up the space within the outer enclosure, thus giving some idea of the vast number of people who once lived on the premises of major Khmer shrines.

79

Originally the main approach was directly from the south, and a road, one of many built by Jayavarman VII, later connected Phimai with Angkor, 225 kilometres distant, covered in seventeen stages.[61] It is likely that this southern orientation was deliberately chosen by the founder so that the main shrine should face in the direction of the capital. This is an indication that the more normal eastern direction was not necessarily sacrosanct, as also in the case of Preah Vihear and Angkor Vat.

Phimai seems to be the only major surviving Buddhist temple on the Khorat Plateau, although there were probably many minor ones, as suggested by the Buddhist images and sculpture in the Bangkok Museum and the provincial museums of Nakhon Ratchasima (Khorat) and Ubon Ratchathani. However, one gains the impression that the Brahmanical cult generally held sway throughout the provinces as the official religion, except in the far northwestern parts of the empire around the Gulf of Siam, where the Mon population was already Buddhist. One must note also that much of the decorative imagery at Phimai is

Hindu, primarily scenes from the Râmâyana. Conventional
Buddhist scenes, such as the ineffectual attack by Mâra on
the Bodhisattva as he sits in meditation, the final gaining
of enlightenment and his entry into nirvâna, decorate the
upper lintels in the darkness of the inner sanctuary. However, there are several representations of a tantric divinity
in dancing pose. A clue to identification is given by an
inscription that records the rebuilding of this temple and
the setting up of an image of Trailokyavijaya by a local
ruler named Virendrâdhipativarman of Chok Vakula in
1108. Thus it seems likely that this great sanctuary was

64 Ta Muen Thom, built just to the north of the Dangrek Range
(and thus now inside Thailand) was once an important stronghold
on the main route from Angkor to Khmer temple-fortresses further
north such as Phnom Rung and Phimai. It has suffered disastrously
from destructive looting by warring soldiery during the past twenty
years or so, but as can be seen from the photograph, the Fine Arts
Department of the Government of Thailand, has recently started
restoration work. Meanwhile, in early 1999 ancient Khmer temples
within Cambodia are still being looted by local military commanders.
See below.

developed as a Buddhist site solely on the initiative of this presumably local governor of the province. Although this particular image referred to is no longer evident, it is likely that the 10-armed dancing figures whom we see represented, particularly on the lintel at the entrance to the main sanctuary and even more clearly reproduced on a lintel in the north-east corner of the galleries, should be identified as Trailokyavijaya ("Victory over the threefold world").[62] This title pertains to Vajrapâni as the result of his subduing and converting to Buddhism the major divinities of the whole (threefold) world, thus forming them into a special mandala known as the *Trilokaçakramandala* (*Mandala of the Circle of the Triple World*), of which he himself is the central presiding divinity.[63]

Ta Muen Thom deserves special mention for two reasons. First, the actual site of this temple near the pass across the Dangrek Range seems to have been fixed by the presence of a jutting stone with a roundish base, which suggests the form of a "self-existent" (*svayambhû*) linga. It was precisely over this that the central shrine with its antechamber was raised. Like Phimai, the main shrine faces south towards Angkor. Since space on the summit on which the whole complex stands is limited, this results in an unusually steep ascent up to the southern and main entrance (*gopura*). The main shrine is flanked by the ruins of subsidiary buildings to left and right, as well as (originally) two towers set back towards the northern side of the courtyard. Thus the essential plan of the temple corresponds to the typical Khmer arrangement of a central towering shrine, flanked by two others of slightly lesser height. Here though the two subsidiary tower-shrines are set rather far back.

The second reason for mentioning this temple is that it illustrates the appalling damage which the cultural heritage of the Khmer Empire has suffered during recent times. Although it lies just inside the present Thai frontier, it was held by the Khmer Rouge after they were driven into this frontier area during the Vietnamese occupation of Cambodia (1979 onwards). All carvings, especially lintels, of value to antique dealers in Bangkok were removed or

65 The entrance to the main shrine at Prâsâd Sikhoraphum on the Khorat plateau. The torana is very fine indeed, showing a 10-armed Íiva dancing on a pedestal consisting of sacred geese (hamsa). This rests upon the usual Kâla mask with an elaborate garland issuing from both sides of its mouth. Note the apsaras to either side of the doorway. The birds which stand on their shoulders seem to be an unusual feature, but we noted a similar image at Bantay Chmar.

seriously damaged in the attempts at removal. Even dynamite was used, resulting in the toal collapse of two of the towers. Since 1991 the Fine Arts Department of the Thai Government has brought welcome order into the resulting chaos, but inevitably the carved stone-work remains irreplaceable.[64]

The beautiful little temple at Sikhoraphum, halfway between Surin and Sisaket on the main railway line travelling east from Khorat, has the same general design typical of a Khmer temple-mountain, *viz.* a major central shrine with four smaller shrines to the four corners. It is set within a square moat and a square walled enclosure. Apart from the charm of the site, it is remarkable for the well preserved lintel over the eastern entrance to the main shrine and for the upper parts of the towers, which represent later non-Khmer developments, as in the Wat Mahathat at Lopburi. The lintel has an elaborate pattern, showing a *kâla*-mask below, surmounted by a dancing Śiva as well as a complicated looping of garlands, incorporating minor divinities and *rishis* (Hindu sages).

83

These temples are but a few examples, albeit the more spectacular ones, of the vast number that cover the Khorat Plateau and areas further westwards around the Gulf of Siam.

During Sûryavarman II's reign several other small temples, all Brahmanical, were built at Angkor. Two, known nowadays as Thammanon and Chau-say-tevoda, stand on either side of the road a short distance beyond the eastern exit from the centre of Angkor Thom, and another, the Preah Pithu, consists of a group of five small temples set well back from the road to the right as one leaves the palace compound towards the northern exit of Angkor Thom.

Thammanon is relatively simple, consisting of a courtyard with entrance portals east and west, a single main shrine preceded by a separate antechamber, and a small building of the kind usually described as a "library". It was restored substantially during the 1920s and displays some excellent carved stone-work, mainly floral designs with inset images of celestial maidens (*apsara*) and guardians. It

66 *A section of a set of 37 small Buddha images subsequently carved around the upper internal walls of one of the originally Śaivite shrines (the highest of the group) known as Preah Pithu (early 12ᵗʰ century). The ushnîsha (top-knot) style shows Thai characteristics and is probably as late as the 16ᵗʰ century when the Khmer court returned to Angkor for a while, and various earlier Khmer structures were adapted to Buddhist use.*

may have been dedicated to Vishnu, who rides Garuda on the frontal piece (*torana*) on the west side of main shrine. Chau-say-tevoda, a Śaivite temple now in an advanced state of ruin, consisted of a single main shrine preceded by a linked antechamber standing in a square courtyard with entrance portals to the four quarters. Some carvings of themes drawn from the Râmâyana still remain to be seen.

Preah Pithu consists of a group of five temples; three of them are of similar design, namely a central shrine in a square courtyard with entrances to the four quarters. They are placed more or less in a row from west to east. Much ruined, they still contain some fine carvings, while others lie strewn around the site. The last in the row, the furthest into the surrounding forest, is particularly interesting, in that the summit shrine was later used as a small Buddhist sanctuary and now 37 small Buddha-images, arranged on a frieze, gaze down on one from above. The number 37 recalls to my mind the set of 37 confessional Buddhas, as found in Tibetan Buddhist tradition, surely of Indian origin, but I remain unaware of any such reference.[65] The fourth temple, north of the other three, had no enclosure but is approached by a fine causeway with *nâga* railings, now in a very dilapidated condition. The fifth temple, the smallest of all, consists of a single shrine with an entrance-hall, linked to the shrine by a vestibule or covered hall, the typical design, one may note, of so many simple Indian shrines.

Angkor Vat, presumed to be the major wonder of the whole Angkor area, impresses by its enormous size. Viewed from a distance it appears at its best, and doubtless at its very best if viewed from the air, when its precise mandala layout set within its square moat can be fully appreciated. Once inside its massive walls, one may well have a feeling of dull monotony. The intricate floral designs which cover the stone-work, a vast labour indeed, lighten one's feelings in no way, and the celestial maidens (*apsaras*), all looking so much the same, whom one meets at every corner, do little to gladden the heart. In so far as this vast temple may be considered as the mausoleum of Sûryavarman II, gloomy sentiments of such a kind may not be unsuitable.

85

Like other temple-mountains, more modest in design, it is laid out like a mandala. It rises on three levels, each terrace more or less identical with towers at the four corners and portals piercing the four sides. Five towers with the central one higher than the others crown the top terrace, which is square. The lower terraces protrude westwards in order to make room for the grandiose western entrance and the two "libraries" to left (north) and right (south) on the second terrace, and for a further hall of approach on the lowest platform. A long causeway crossing the moat and passing between two subsidiary buildings, likewise referred to as "libraries", finally brings one to this grand entrance, after which gloom prevails until one has climbed to the highest pinnacles to appreciate the truly magnificent views.

The bas-reliefs present eight major subjects, two to each side of the four major entrance portals, and a large number of small individual scenes decorating the walls of the corner towers. All these smaller scenes and most of the main subjects are drawn straight from the Indian epics, and most treat of war and the triumph of battle. The exceptions are the Churning of the Ocean by Gods and Demons in order to gain the Elixir of Life, and the illustration of the paths to Heaven and Hell. Even in the case of these paths, one cannot but have the impression that those on the way to Heaven—even riding horses—are the victors of war, while those being cudgelled on the way to future sufferings are the wretched losers who are being driven into captivity.

Going round in anti-clockwise direction from the western entrance we see: (1) the great war between the Pandavas and the Kauravas from the Mahâbhârata, (2) Sûryavarman II triumphant and in military array, (3) Heaven and Hell scenes, (4) the Churning of the Ocean, (5) the crushing victory of Vishnu over the demons, (6) the victory of Krishna over the demon Bana, (7) the war of the victorious gods over the demons, and (8) the battle of Lanka from the Râmâyana.

A few interesting details may be added. No. 6 consists of a series of scenes in which Krishna in an eight-headed and eight-armed manifestation, mounted on Garuda, appears several times. He is assisted by Agni, god of fire, who rides a rhinoceros, a rare animal to see on these panels. No. 7 presents the major gods of Hindu mythology, each riding his appropriate mount while subduing one of the demons. From left to right one may recognise Kubera, god of wealth, riding a *yaksha*, Skanda, god of war, riding a peacock, Indra, riding his elephant, then the centrepiece, namely Vishnu on Garuda battling with the Demon Kâlanemi, next Yama, god of death, in a chariot drawn by bulls, Śiva drawing his bow, Brahma on his sacred goose, Sûrya, god of the sun, issuing from the sun-disk, and

Varuna, god of the waters, riding a *nâga*.[66]

This vast "temple-mountain" was dedicated as *Paramavishnuloka*, the "Supreme World of Vishnu", this being the posthumous name of Sûryavarman II. It is assumed that he was entombed here with the result that Angkor Vat may also be regarded as a mausoleum. This explains adequately why it faces west instead of east. One may compare Çandi Jago in East Java, which was also intended as a mausoleum and thus faces west.[67]

One other rarely visited temple-fortress is Beung Mialia (the "Garlanded Pool"), situated some 40 kilomentres north-east of Angkor below the eastern flank of Phnom

67 Bantay Samre (Angkor), of which one sees here the eastern approach, resembles a small citadel with its massive walls of laterite, constructed double on the other three sides. Founded about the middle of the 12th century, it follows the regular pattern of a main central shrine, of which the tiered roof is clearly visible, approached by a spacious mandapa *(antechamber), the whole complex being enclosed within an inner courtyard with massive portals to the four directions. On the eastern side of this courtyard are two supplementary buildings, conventionally referred to as libraries. As a normal Śaivite shrine, it contained a central linga, while the several* toranas *depict mainly scenes from the Ramâyâna epic. Details of its foundation are unknown, but its name associates it with the Samre clan, an aboriginal people who live in the Phnom Kulen area.*

Kulen. This Brahmanical temple, datable by its style to about the mid-12th century, must be among the last complexes on a grand style constructed before the great monuments of Jayavarman VII began to dominate Angkor. A visit to Beung Mia-lia, described in detail in Maurice Glaize's *Les Monuments du groupe d'Angkor* (pp.277-80), can be combined with a visit to Phnom Kulen, although it is impracticable to cover the whole in one day. It lies off a side-road, ascending towards the eastern flank of Phnom Kulen, that leads off from a new highway, linking Dongdaik eventually to Anlong Veng. Close to the village of the same name, presumably originally embraced within this enormous complex, which is over four kilometres in circumference, stands the central temple-fortress, consisting of three enclosed courtyards, a rectangle measuring about 250 by 180 metres. The interior is in such an advanced state of delapidation that one clambers over massive blocks of fallen sandstone, while the whole structure is buried in jungle. There is a little or no decoration except on the frontal pieces over the doorways, representing the great Hindu divinites or scenes from the Râmâyana. A general impression of this central area may be given by comparing it with the far smaller and far better preserved Bantay Samre at Angkor.

Mention must also be made at this point of Prâsâd Narai Jaeng Vaeng since it dates probably to about the mid-11th century and has the distinction of being the most northerly of Khmer temples known in Thailand. All that survives is the tower of the main shrine, but this is remarkably well preserved while having the aesthetic advantage of standing in the beautiful grounds of the Theravâdin monastery of the same name. The *torana* is adorned with a multi-armed figure of dancing Śiva, while an image of Vishnu lying on his side surmounts the lintel on the northern side of the shrine. This lintel shows Krishna killing a lion, while that on the eastern side shows him fighting with a pair of lions. The seeming remoteness of this Khmer temple far to the north probably derives from the lack of archaeological research in this area. Another ancient

68 Prâsâd Narai Jaeng Vaeng on the outskirts of Sakhon Nakhon (north-east Thailand). The name in Khmer (with variant Thai spelling) appears to be an old nickname meaning "Narayan (Vishnu) with long legs" referring to an image of a prostate Vishnu above the lintel on the northern side. This temple of which only the main shrine with its well preserved tower stills remains, stands in the grounds of the later Theravâdin monastery of the same name. There appears to be no trace of the rest of the whole temple enclosure of which this was once the centre. It probably dates from the period of the grandiose building activities of Sûryavarman I and has the distinction of being the most northerly survival of Khmer temple architecture. A fine torana of a dancing Śiva surmounts the lintel on the east side. More details are given in the text.

Khmer monument, seemingly of slender proportions, remains enshrined in the great stûpa of the main Theravâdin
monastery of Phrathat Cheun Chum in the centre of
Sakhon Nakhon. This can be seen through small ornamental windows, conveniently left ajar, to the four sides
of this impressive "Laos-style" shrine, but in the course of
our brief visit to this pleasant north-eastern Thai city it
proved impossible to gain closer access.[68] On the eastern
limits of the town there is yet another Khmer temple,
known as Phrathat Dum, of which only the central tower
of the original three brick-built towers is still standing.

Returning to our historical survey, we note that
Sûryavarman II disappears from the scene c. 1150 and is
succeeded by a cousin, possibly as the result of a palace
revolution, who was crowned as Dharanîndravarman II and
probably reigned from 1150 to 1160. Little is known about
him except that he was a Buddhist, and later his son, who
brought order to the greatly troubled empire, was crowned
as Jayavarman VII, the one great Khmer ruler to build lav-
ish Buddhist monuments.

90

In the meantime, Yaśovarman II (1160-65/66), who
succeeded Dharanîndravarman, was overthrown by a
usurper. For the next ten years Angkor was subjected to
continual assaults by the Chams, culminating with the
great sea invasion of 1177. Except for the fortuitous removal of the usurper, this was the greatest calamity that
befell Angkor until the Thai invasions two centuries later.
On this occasion the Chams attacked by sea, sailing round
the coast, then up the Mekong River, the Ton-le Sap and
the Great Lake, thus taking Angkor by surprise. They
burned and pillaged the city, carrying off vast booty and
herding prisoners into slavery. It may well be said that
Sûryavarman and his successors brought this retribution
upon themselves by their continual harassing of the Chams.

At the time of the revolution that brought the usurper
to power, the future Jayavarman VII was even then in the
process of conducting a campaign against the Cham capital of Vijaya (Binh-dinh), whence he had hastily returned,
presumably to secure his right to the succession. Thus it

now fell to him to restore order in the kingdom, and for the next few years he waged war by land and on sea against the Chams. The successful sea-battles were later depicted on the walls of his major architectural creation, the Bayon. He was crowned in 1181 and in the twenty years or so of his reign he did more for the greater glory of Angkor than any previous ruler. Apart from the ruins of the Baphuon and the Phimea-akas, and a few lesser temples, Angkor Thom ("Great Angkor") as we see it in its ruined state today is essentially the city as recreated by Jayavarman VII, while the great Buddhist temple-complexes outside the walls, such as Bantay Kdei, Ta Prohm and Preah Khan, as well as the smaller ones such as Preah Palilay, Ta Nei, Ta Som, and Neak Poen, even the lesser known Krol Ko, Bantay Prei and Prâsâd Prei, are all attributable in one way or another to his reign.

A major task was to redefine the area of the city and to this purpose new city walls were built, forming a square three kilometres on each side, protected by a moat 100 metres across. Four roads radiated from the centre of his reconstructed city, now marked by his temple mountain, the Bayon, while the earlier road eastwards from the palace towards Ta Keo was retained, thus resulting in five great gateways, each surmounted by the benevolent (or warning) gaze of the Bodhisattva Avalokiteśvara, presumably identified with the king himself, facing in all four directions. They are approached from the outside with a causeway, of which the "railings" consist of *nâgas*, held as if in a tug-of-war between giant figures, the gods to one side and the demons (*asura*) to the other. Whatever other significance may be attached to this formation, it is scarcely possible to dissociate it from the well known story of the Churning of the Ocean by the gods and the demons, especially as both "teams" are represented here. Jayavarman VII also built "corner shrines" (Prâsâd Chrung) at the four angles (SE, NE, NW, SW) of the massive city-walls. In front of the palace grounds he constructed the imposing terrace, 300 metres long, presumably a royal vantage point for parades and formal receptions. The whole length is decorated with carved scenes of elephant riders, with *garudas* and rampant lions and even scenes of sport.

During Jayavarman's manifold building operations – the reconstructed city, roads linking Angkor to other major centres throughout the "empire", rest-houses along these same roads, hospitals and monastic foundations, and probably lastly his own "temple-mountain", the Bayon – he was also engaged in a war of revenge against Champa. Jayavarman employed as his "commanding general" in this campaign a refugee Cham prince, named Vidyânandana, to whose education and training he gave special care, but having achieved the subjugation of Champa, this prince carved out a kingdom for himself, first as a kind of acknowledged dependent and then in armed revolt against his benefactor. However, with the co-operation of the uncle of this ungrateful client, Jayavarman once more turned the situation to his advantage, and thus Champa remained subject to Angkor throughout the rest of his reign, and even until 1220.[69]

Meanwhile Angkor's hold on the western provinces, southern Thailand and the upper Thai-Malay peninsula, was maintained and even extended. More Buddhist shrines were built in Lopburi, of which the most imposing is Wat Mahathat, consisting of a central shrine set within two square walled enclosures. The central shrine with its "corn-cob" profile is purely Khmer of this late period, similar to other great shrines on the Khorat Plateau, but the surrounding shrines are mainly later reconstructions. The Prang Sam Yod consists of the typical Khmer arrangement of three shrines of which the centre one predominates, just as we have noted from Ruluos (Hariharâlâya) onwards.

Although the temples built during the reign of Jayavarman VII, when Buddhism at long last becomes the proclaimed religion of the state, were often Buddhist in intention, Brahmanical influences do not disappear either at the court or in the decorations of these temples, where Hindu motifs continue to intrude. The extreme limit westwards of the Khmer Empire at this time is indicated by the ruins of the Buddhist temple of Muang Singh ("Victorious

69 A Khmer temple-tower, still standing in Wat Kampaeng Leng in Phetchaburi, Thailand, some 165 kms south of Bangkok. The Khmers were well established down the Peninsula as far as Chaiya in the 11th and 12th centuries. It has the same "corncob" appearance as similar Khmer-style towers built in Lopburi and elsewhere in Thailand.

Lion") near modern Kanchanaburi, some 120 kilometres west of present-day Bangkok. This seems to have been a walled citadel, similar in layout to Phimai, dating from the late 12th to early 13th century.[70]

Moving south down the peninsula we reach the last of Khmer temple building at Phetchaburi,where substantial temple-ruins of the 11th to 12th centuries bear witness to earlier Khmer suzerainty. Khmer influence eventually reached as far south as Chaiya near Ligor (Nakhon Si

Thammarat), where the population was doubtless Malay. The inscription on an image set up there in 1183 by the Governor of Chaiya in the name of the Mahârâja of Śrîvijaya was written in Khmer. He may have intended this as a declaration, to be clearly understood by the Khmers that this was properly a Śrîvijayan domain (See my *Asian Commitment*, p. 386).

It was within this context of outright war on the eastern front and holding operations to the west that the various building works of Jayavarman VII proceeded. We may consider first the major monastic complexes of Preah Khan, outside the walls of the city and slightly to the north-east, Ta Prohm and its close neighbour Bantay Kdei, both outside the walls towards the south-east, and other associated temples. At that time there were lakes on all sides. To the east of Bantay Kdei there is still the very beautiful Sra Srang, a rectangular pool approximately 700 by 300 metres, probably constructed during an earlier reign. Ta Prohm on its northern side abutted onto the already existing Eastern Baray. Preah Khan was newly provided with a large artificial lake, known as the *Jayatatâka*, on its eastern side, nearly half the length of the Eastern Baray, and also a smaller lake on its western side. Preah Khan would have been reached on its main eastern side by boat, and the foundations of the landing site are still there to be seen.

94

In the middle of this larger lake Jayavarman later built the delightful little shrine known as Neak Poen, and on its far eastern shore the smaller monastery of Ta Som. Close to the northern shores of the *Jayatatâka* the small monastic compound of Bantay Prei was founded together with the nearby temple of Prâsâd Prei, while further eastwards, still close to the shore of the lake, the monastic compound of Krol Ko was built. As one drives around these various ruined sites nowadays, it is difficult to recreate in one's mind the charm and splendour of these various magnificent buildings, surrounded by vast stretches of water and interconnected by a network of canals. One reads of the wonder of Angkor, but with the disappearance of these vast water-works, not only was the prosperity of the city

70 Rows of decorative stone posts form an avenue on the main approaches to Preah Khan, built by Jayavarman VII in honour of his father and probably also as a personal residence on the site of a victorious battle against the invading Chams soon after 1181. An image of Avalokiteßvara, representing his father, was erected there in 1193. As can be seen, these posts originally showed deeply cut images of small meditating Buddhas on their upper sections. Only one or two remain, as they were deliberately defaced as the result a strong Brahmanical reaction at court during the mid-13th century. However as will be learned from the text, Buddhism was by then already established as the more popular religion throughout the empire.

lost for ever, but also much of that wonder.

The grounds of the temple-complex of Preah Khan ("Sacred Sword") form a rectangle of 700 by 800 metres,

71 The so-called "dancers' hall" in the eastern precincts of Preah Khan, the great temple complex built by Jayavarman VII in honour of his father. This hall, nicknamed thus because of the frieze of dancing figures, is 6.40 metres square and appears to be the largest known stone-roofed structure in the whole of Angkor. As the Khmers never mastered the building of a true arch, the width of their structures was limited by the maximum balancing weight of a corbelled roof, viz. constructed of overlapping stones.

presumably filled originally with lesser buildings for its population of about 14,000 persons. Now all is forest except for the central rectangle (175 by 200 metres) of the second enclosure. This too before its clearance earlier this century was likewise buried in jungle. The main complex is now cleared of undergrowth and the passage through it is easy. Preah Khan differs from the other Buddhist temple-complexes in that the entrances from all four directions are preceded by causeways with "railings" consisting of *nâgas* pulled by giant figures, on exactly the same pattern as already described for the main city of Angkor Thom itself. This suggests that Jayavarman himself may have used it, perhaps in the earlier part of his reign, as his private residence. An important inscription found in 1939 provided much detailed information concerning the foundation of this royal abode.[71]

In this place of victory in combat, which was a receptacle of enemy blood, he established this city of which the stones and the golden lotus-flowers vary the colour of the soil, which shines still today as though glazed with blood.

97

If Prayâga (the Indian city of Allahabad) is worthy of respect because of the proximity of two holy rivers (the Ganges and the Jumna) which provide means for the purification for living beings, what should be said of this city of Jayasrî with its watering places (tîrtha) where Buddha, Śiva and the Lotus-Eyed One are invoked.

This King Jayavarman has consecrated here in the Year Śaka 1113 (= AD1192) this Lokeśa (Lord of the World) named Lord Jayavarman, who is the image of his father.

Around this sacred Avalokiteśvara who is central, the King has placed 283 divine images.

This certainly suggests that this temple was built on the site of a battle, presumably when the invading Chams were being driven from the capital by Jayavarman himself, hence its construction as both a vast Buddhist temple in honour of his father and himself and also as a city of "Glorious victory" (*Jayasrî*), as remembered by the more popular name of the "Sacred Sword", which survives to this day.

The general lay-out resembles that of the "temple-mountain". It consists of a central tower-like shrine with similar but slightly lower towers to the four quarters, enclosed within a double inner courtyard, which is again enclosed within the more spacious outer courtyard with elaborate towered porticoes and antechambers. But there is the essential difference that while the "temple-mountains" soar upwards, these Buddhist temples spread out on a horizontal plane, thus conforming closely to the regular mandala pattern. The inner enclosure is a maze of small shrines connected by the usual narrow covered galleries, as typical of all these massive Khmer buildings. On account of their exclusive use of corbelled archways, the overbearing weight inevitably limits the span available. In this respect one should mention the antechamber on the eastern side, nicknamed the Dancers' Hall because of the frieze of dancing *apsaras* which decorate the upper walls. This is the widest spanned hall with corbelled roof in the whole of Angkor.[72]

There was no difference in architectural design of these vast temples, whether Śaivite, Vishnuite or as now nominally Buddhist. The cult would have been identical, but one assumes that Buddhist monks would have co-operated with Brahman priests at the various shrines, living in their separate communities on the vast estate enclosed by the outer walls. The items required for the cult are all listed, such as rice, sesame, milk, honey, molasses, and the quantities expected, followed by the numbers of animals and people attached to the temple:

423 goats, 360 pigeons, as many peacocks and yellow-green pigeons (Colomba hurriyala). In his devotion the King has given 5,324 villages with their inhabitants, totalling 978,840 men and women, among whom there are 444 officials, 4,006 attendants, cooks and others, 2,298 of the servile class, including 1,000 dancers, and 7,436 persons responsible for the temple-oblations.

The total number of residents seems to amount to about 14,000. One may well wonder how much practical Buddhism was involved amongst this vast concourse, but at least the inscription in its conventional opening verses is generally Buddhist Mahâyâna in its worthy intentions. It treats in turn the Buddha (in his three phases of manifestation according to Mahâyâna theory), the Dharma (understood here as the Way of the Bodhisattva) and the

Sangha (the community of monks). These are three pillars of Buddhism.

The Lord who by his accumulations (of knowledge and merit) produces on a vast scale bodily forms of the Dharma-Body, the Glorious Body and the Transformation Body, let him be adored, he who is the harbour of Buddhas and those who embody the nature of Buddhas (viz. Bodhisattvas), to Buddha who is the refuge of living beings be praise!

I honour the Way of the incomparable Supreme Enlightenment, the one and only untrammelled doctrine for the elucidation of absolute being, the Dharma, worthy of praise as the praiseworthy immortality known throughout the Threefold World, like a sword which cuts away the obscurity of the six internal foes (of desire, wrath, greed, delusion, pride and envy).

May the Sangha (community of monks), outstanding in their intent upon the good, lead you! (The Sangha) is freed from attachment since this obstructs final deliverance, but it is always intent on the advantage of others, whom they instruct in the Buddha's teachings, which they themselves recite together.

These identical Sanskrit verses serve as opening to the inscription on the stone which records details concerning the great Buddhist temple of Ta Prohm, so maybe they are largely conventional.

99

The outer walls of Ta Prohm, enclosing an area of one kilometre by 600 metres, once contained a population of 12,640 persons. This included 418 chief officials, with a further 2,740 on their staff, 2,232 retainers of the serving class including 615 female dancers. Furthermore, 66,625 men and women (presumably the supporting villagers) provide the services for the gods, totalling 79,365, with the Burmese and Chams presumably pressed into service. The inscription, dated AD1186, records that Jayavarman founded this temple-complex as the city of Râjavibhâra, setting up here an image named Srî Jayarâjaçûdâmani, representing his mother as the Mother of the Buddhas (namely *Prajñâpâramitâ*, the Perfection of Wisdom), as well as two other images to left and right, representing his revered teachers (*guru*), surrounded by an entourage of 260 divinities.

No special features attach to the approaches to this temple-complex, except that the entrance portals to all four quarters are surmounted by the four-faced gaze of

Avalokiteśvara, just like the main city portals, but on a smaller scale. The layout of the Ta Prohm temple-complex itself generally resembles that of Preah Khan, but the large number of fig-trees that intertwine amongst the walls make it more difficult to penetrate the inner courtyards and corridors. All this provides, however, an idealized impression of "ancient Angkor lost in the jungle".

Despite its large enclosure of 700 by 500 metres, the temple-complex of Bantay Kdei is appreciably smaller, being only 63 by 50 metres. Also no attempt has been made here to maintain a symmetrical mandala pattern. Within this inner enclosure we find a generally rectangular arrangements of tower-like shrines positioned rather towards the

72 A side view of Bantay Kdei. As observed in the text, it is impossible to gain any general view of the two major temple-palaces built by Jayavarman VII, namely Preah Khan in honour of his father and Ta Prohm in honour of his mother. Both are surrounded by dense jungle. In the case of a third such temple-palace, namely Bantay Kdei, of which no inscription reveals the intention, it is possible to gain a fine view, especially from the southern side across the moat which surrounds the second enclosure. In this photograph one can see the central shrine, seeming as though flanked by the massive gopuras of the first (inner) enclosure to the north and the south, while to the right one sees the inner eastern gopura.

east, as the normal direction of approach. Although described by Maurice Glaize as the least engaging of these three temple-complexes, I have always found it the most attractive. It is impossible to appreciate the others from ground-level because of the density of jungle that surrounds them, but one can view Bantay Kdei from its southern side, where the trees are far less dense, and admire the series of towers which rise in harmony beyond the walls of the inner enclosure. The twisting floral designs and pairs of dancing *apsaras* that decorate the walls and the pillars also seem to relate closely to the Bayon. Inset deeply cut figures of guardians and *apsaras* are now a general feature of all these later temples.

Mention must be made of the shrines closely associated with Preah Khan, all easily reached in earlier times by boat from the eastern pier. The temple known popularly as Neak Poen, because of the two *nâgas* which encircle the base of the circular shrine, is set in the centre of its own square lake, the whole complex forming an island in the middle of the much larger *Jayatatâka*. It seems to have been conceived in imitation of the quasi-mythical Anavatapta Lake in the high Himalayas, renowned for its pure cool (*anavatapta*) waters. It is famous in Tibetan tradition and closely associated with Avalokiteśvara, who appears depicted on the sides of this small shrine. Thus the colophon of the *Blue Annals*, a major 15th-century Tibetan historical work by the Scholar gZhon-nu-dpal, refers to:

101

the Land of Snows (Tibet), resting on the golden foundation of the blessing of the Great Merciful Lord (Avalokiteśvara), surrounded by majestic snow mountains, where eternal streams of monks from the Anavatapta Lake of Morality, which removes the heat of defilement, make it replete with the jewels of preaching and meditation.

Despite the mixed metaphors, this expresses admirably the religious and the healing associations of this lake, which in the case of Neak Poen has four subsidiary shrines to the four sides of this inner pool, where the faithful might take the beneficial waters, and indeed still do today. Upper panels on three sides of the central shrine depict main scenes form the life of Śâkyamuni Buddha: his flight from the palace, the cutting of his hair as a sign of renouncing a worldly life (the only one which remains clearly distinguishable), and his mediation under the Tree of Enlightenment. The southern panel, entirely defaced, probably illustrated his entry into final nirvâna. The statue of the horse on the eastern side of the shrine is said to represent Avalokiteśvara hastening to the salvation of sentient beings.

The temple of Ta Som, near the eastern shore of the Jayatatâka, resembles a small version of Bantay Kdei. It stands within a double enclosure and the main entrance portals are crowned with the four-faced glance of Avalokiteśvara. Although ruined in its interior it retains some fine detailed carving on the towers of the various shrines, primarily miniature row of devotees in the act of supplication.

On the northern side of the lake in close proximity to Preah Khan one should visit Prasat Prei (the "Forest Sanctuary") and just behind it Bantay Prei (the "Forest Citadel"), and also Krol Ko (nicknamed now the "Cow Enclosure") further along the same northern side of the lake, for despite their much ruined condition, the total tranquillity of these sites urges one to linger. The ruined towers stand solitary amongst the broken walls and collapsed masonry, interspersed with carved plaques which have been set in position to form ordered rows. One is thus totally released from the gloom of the interiors of better preserved temples.

Similar in layout to Ta Som but rather different in atmosphere, the temple known as Ta Nei was built in proximity to the western shore of the Eastern Baray. It is now reached by a footpath, nearly one kilometre from the main road of the so called "Inner Circuit" between Ta Keo and Ta Prohm. Ta Nei stands abandoned in the jungle with its walls reasonably cleared of vegetation. Like Ta Som it retains some fine carving, including a plaque of the Bodhisattva, the future Buddha Śâkyamuni, fleeing from the palace on his horse. Penetrating deeper amongst the trees towards the east one comes upon the well preserved eastern portal with a fine raised carving of Avalokiteśvara,

102

standing on a lotus-flower.

Another seldom visited temple-fortress, presumably built under the orders of Jayavarman VII, is Bantay Thom (Great), situated about 3 kilometres north-west of the city. It is reached by a narrow sandy track leading off from the "Outer Circuit", just beyond the northern gateway of Angkor Thom. Quite possibly it was conceived as an out-post as part of the new defensive arrangements instituted by Jayavarman VII, able to give warning of any hostile approach from this direction. Much delapidated, its three central towers still stand, although not for much longer unless urgent restoration work begins soon. These stand in an inner rectangular couryard of 34 by 43 metres, en-closed within an outer courtyard of 104 by 116 metres. Two so-called "libraries", much ruined, stood in the usual position just inside the eastern gateway to the inner court-yard. Apart from the expected decoration of *apsaras* and guardian-divinities set in their individual niches, there is some exquisitely decorative stonework on the towers. Es-pecially noteworthy are several well preserved lintels, one of the Bodhisattva (the future Śâkyamuni) fleeing from his palace at night, as already noticed at Ta Nei, and an-other of Mahâmâya, his mother, honoured by a pair of el-ephant-riders and attendant divinities. Situated on a slight eminence in desolate open brushland, this site would re-main impressive for this reason alone. My thanks are due to Mr Kong Samsara of the office of the Conservation d'Angkor in Siem Reap, who accompanied Vutthy and myself on this visit, providing me also with the precise measurements just given.

103

Within the city walls there is one Buddhist temple of note, apart from the Bayon. This is Preah Palilay, which is found amongst the trees just north of the palace grounds. Unhappily it is now so dilapidated that its original form as a single tower-like shrine, open to all four directions and raised on a multi-tiered terrace, is now scarcely recogniz-able. However, some finely carved Buddhist scenes can still be seen on the upper sections of the sides of the sole eastern portico (*gopura*). Still clearly visible are the scenes of

73 A torana *from Bantay Thom, illustrating the flight of the Bodhisattva (the future Śâkyamuni) from his palace at night on his horse Kanthaka in order to follow an ascetic life against the orders of his father.*

74 Another torana *from Bantay Thom, not so easily identified. As this is clearly a Buddhist temple it may well represent Mahâmâya, his royal mother, standing beneath the tree under which she gave birth, flanked by elephant riders who are bringing their charges to perform the necessary ablutions in accordance with the traditional account of the Bodhisattva's birth. The two divinities who were present at the scene were Brâhma and Indra, and these may be represented by the two capped figures. The style of workmanship recalls that of Steung. I found both these pieces stolen on a subsequent visit.*

Śâkyamuni receiving the dish of curds offered him by the village-girl Sujâtâ, and the scene where he tames the fierce elephant sent to destroy him by his jealous cousin Devadatta. Another scene, less clear, illustrates the offerings of animals of the forests, monkeys, elephants and peacocks.[73]

Apart from the new or reconstructed buildings in Angkor itself, many other sites throughout the empire were renovated and new temples initiated. Mention has already been made of those at Lopburi, at Muang Singh, at Phimai, Phnom Rung and Sikhoraphum. To these one might well add Ku Suan Taeng and Kamphaeng Yai with its nearby "hospital chapel", known as Kamphaeng Noi, which are among the most northerly of the Khmer shrines remaining on the Khorat Plateau.[74] As already mentioned above in the case of Phimai, several of these sites were connected by roads with "hospitals" and "rest-houses" at various places. Clearly these were all constructed of less robust materials, but the attached "chapels" built of stone have survived. A good example in Angkor itself may be seen just inside the eastern precincts of Preah Khan. Another one of easy access if visiting Phnom Rung is to be found at the foot of a hill a few hundred metres from Muang Tam. A well preserved one is found at Bantay Chmar, and another in a beautiful forest setting on the way to Ta Muen Thom. Foundation steles show that these beneficent works were dedicated to the Buddha Master of Medicine (*Bhaishajyaguru*), also well known in Tibet.

105

One of the last important shrines surrounded by city-walls like Phimai is Bantay Chmar, dedicated to Jayavarman VII's son Indravarman. Originally built on the main route from Angkor towards the western provinces of the Khmer empire around the Gulf of Siam, it still lies just within the present Cambodian frontier, some 60 kilometres north of the town of Sisophon, almost a three-hour journey because of the condition of the road. As this region has been under military occupation of one kind or another during the last two decades and more, it was possible to visit this interesting site only on chance occasions. Because of its inaccessibility it has never been properly

106

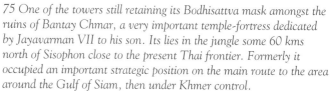
75 One of the towers still retaining its Bodhisattva mask amongst the ruins of Bantay Chmar, a very important temple-fortress dedicated by Jayavarman VII to his son. Its lies in the jungle some 60 kms north of Sisophon close to the present Thai frontier. Formerly it occupied an important strategic position on the main route to the area around the Gulf of Siam, then under Khmer control.

excavated and no great works of renovation have been carried out as at so many other sites. Apart from its obvious strategic and military importance in the past, it is especially interesting as one of the few great enclaves outside Jayavarman VII's recreated city of Angkor that is Bud-

76 A *frieze of dancing figures which decorates the eastern end of the main building at Bantay Chmar, recalling that already illustrated at Preah Khan (Angkor). Here the dancers have a strangely monstrous appearance as though aping the pose of* garuda.

107

77 *Although presumably intended as a Buddhist establishment like all his other great creations, Bantay Chmar like the Bayon shows remarkably little Buddhist imagery. The main figure on this* torana *must surely be identified as a four-headed figure of Brâhma with two geese on one side and two rishis on the other.*

78 *This rather unusual scene for a* torana *seems to represent a group of rishis performing an oblation ceremony. Lamentably the head of the one in prayerful meditation has been hacked off by Khmer soldiery for sale to antique dealers in Bangkok. Bantay Chmar has suffered much damage only recently as described in the text.*

108

dhist in intention. The central enclave, a rectangle of 250 by 200 metres, stood originally at the centre of a far larger area of which the ramparts can be identified, thus enclosing the neat little "hospital chapel", remarkably well pre-

79 *One of the many "hospital chapels", once forming an essential part of the rest-places and hospitals which Jayavarman VII established at the main centres along his newly constructed highways throughout his realm. Such chapels stood amongst other buildings, intended for wayfarers and for the sick, all built of far more fragile materials. This one stands within the outer enclosure, over four kilometres in circumference, of Bantay Chmar, built in the early 13th century on the main route from Angkor to the area of the Gulf of Siam which was then all subject to the Khmers.*

served, as at Preah Khan (Angkor). The outer walls of this central enclave are covered with bas-reliefs, mainly of marches and battle-scenes as on many of the walls of the Bayon, but there was also a remarkable row of full-sized images of a multi-armed Avalokiteśvara, although other Buddhist scenes seem to be absent (again as on the Bayon). Many are so worn and blacked with lichen that to study them in detail is a laborious undertaking, rendered even more difficult by the dense undergrowth which surrounds the whole enclosure. Having penetrated inside these walls, the main structures are now in such a state of ruin that the even the main outlines are scarcely discernable, while progress is hampered by the accumulations of fallen sandstone blocks over which one must clamber and the obstructing undergrowth through which one must force or cut one's way. In effect the central shrine is a long narrow structure, perhaps resembling that of Bantay Kdei at Angkor, with subsidiary buildings linking this to the *gopuras* (ornate entrances) at the four quarters. The eastern one corresponds to the so-called "dancers' hall" at Preah Khan in that its upper level is decorated with a row of dancing female figures which here adopt the rather grotesque pose of a row of *garudas*. One misses the absence of any specifically Buddhist imagery except possibly on the well preserved frontal piece which leads into this particular chamber. Here I would happily have identified the central seated figure as the four-headed image of Vairoçana Buddha, but if so, he is manifestly conceived as a four-headed Brahma with a rishi playing a lute on his right and a pair of geese on his left. Some of the towers which are still standing retain their Buddha/Bodhisattva heads, as at the Bayon and Preah Khan. Like many other sites in Cambodia, Bantay Chmar has suffered depredation at the hands of the groups of soldiers who have been occupying the region. [75]

With good reason doubts have been raised whether Jayavarman VII within the course of a reign of twenty years could possibly have been responsible for such a vast building programme. He must have operated with enormous work-forces, completely overtaxing the economy of the country, which suffered accordingly. It is generally agreed that his last great work was that of his own "temple-mountain", the Bayon.

Although unusually complex in its final form, the Bayon conforms to the normal mandala pattern of the earlier temple-mountains. There is the central tower-like shrine, open to the four directions, on a circular raised terrace, surrounded by similar but lower tower-like shrines to the four directions. These lower shrines appear as duplicated on the eastern side (the main side of approach) because of the elaborate *loggia*, which leads up to the main shrine. Similar tower-like shrines stand in the four intermediate directions. From the summit of each Avalokiteśvara likewise gazes in all four directions. This main complex lies within a square enclosure, adorned by sixteen tower-like shrines, one at each corner and three on each side, each tower surmounted by four-faced Avalokiteśvara. We thus

110

80 *A view of the Bayon, taken from the west side. This is the major creation of Jayavarman VII, constructed in the form of a raised mandala with subsidiary towers to the four quarters and the four intermediate quarters. All bear the face of Avalokiteśvara, identified with Jayavarman VII himself, gazing in the four directions The outer and inner enclosures, of which the western outer enclosure may be seen here, are covered with carved panels, as illustrated below.*

81 Bayon, outer wall, south side towards the west: a procession of elephants escorted by foot-soldiers.

82 Bayon, outer wall, south side towards the east: a kitchen scene.

approximate closely enough to the regular mandala design: the main divinity emanates as four, then eight, and then sixteen. This essential design is then enclosed in a rectangle of 140 by 160 metres, certainly modest in size compared with Angkor Vat. Unfortunately, inside the main enclosure a seeming maze of stone corridors, due to later changes in the design, surround the steps of ascent to the main shrine on all four sides, and here for a short while one stumbles in gloom. However, once on the summit terrace and in brilliant sunlight again, one stands entranced with the now beneficent gazes of Avalokiteśvara, which surround one on all sides.[76]

Bas-reliefs cover most of the exterior walls of the outer and the inner enclosure. They are more deeply cut that those of Angkor Vat and thus far easier to photograph successfully. They are also more varied in content, as though the artisans at work had been given a space to fill with the minimum of instructions. Surprisingly, on these carved panels of a self-proclaimed Buddhist monument, there is not one single Buddhist theme. Is it possible that all artisans were so used to reproducing Hindu themes that they had no Buddhist themes in their repertoire? Although traces of carvings of small Buddha-images can still be seen within the dark galleries of the Bayon and even paintings of Buddhas and other Buddhist divinities on the walls of the inner shrine of Preah Khan, I would surmise that this was largely true at Angkor. Even if these bas-reliefs were completed after the end of Jayavarman VII's reign, there was as yet no overt hostility to his preference for Buddhism. Meanwhile elaborate Buddhist stone carvings were certainly in vogue in the north-western provinces, as is evident from the exhibits of Khmer workmanship in the Bangkok Museum, as well as in the main sanctuary at Phimai.

112

As at Angkor Vat, scenes of war and military parades tend to dominate at the Bayon, interspersed with scenes of daily life, in the palace, in the forest, even ordinary people at work and at play. Beginning at the eastern entrance and going round in the regular clockwise direction, I give a summary of the various themes. Thus we begin on the outer eastern wall (south side) with military parades as the main subject but also with some princesses in a palace and next some ascetics depicted above. The outer southern wall depicts (to the right) the great sea-battle between the Khmers and the Chams, as already mentioned above, and (to the left) military elephant parades, but between these two major scenes we see men engaged in fishing and cock-fighting, a bull-fight and then palace scenes. The outer western wall (starting always from the right) depicts warriors on elephants once again, with scenes of temple-building and life of ascetics above. We then see scenes of fighting and chase with elephants in front, and finally the king returning from a visit (to ascetics) in the forest. The outer northern wall illustrates again scenes of combat with the Chams, while above we see athletes and jugglers, a defile of animals and ascetics in a forest by a river. Finally the eastern wall (north side) shows Khmers and Chams still at war.

The walls of the inner enclosure have far more varied, constantly changing scenes, of which it is difficult to give a coherent account. Here scenes of everyday life and religious scenes predominate. Śiva and Vishnu appear frequently. I give a condensed survey, beginning at the eastern entrance and going in a clockwise direction. First we see a scene of ascetics and animals in a forest, Brahmans presumably performing a ceremony around a brazier, palace scenes and also a procession of soldiers. The southern wall has again a processions of soldiers and palace scenes. There is a fight between a lion and an elephant, presumably for royal entertainment. There is a large Garuda and a gigantic fish, representing the ocean out of which rises Mount Meru with its ascetics and animals There are musicians and a procession of men carrying an empty throne, a child being put into a coffin, a fisherman in his boat and a large lotus in a pool. These several scenes have been identified as referring to the story of Krishna's son Pradyumna, who was stolen by a demon, thrown into the sea, then swallowed by a large fish which was caught by a fisherman, who cut open the fish and refound the child. Presumably the artisans at work on this section happened to know these scenes well and so introduced them after their own fashion. The southern wall, left side, has scenes of Śiva and Vishnu, a pool with ascetics and animals, palace scenes and possibly a royal pilgrimage. The western wall again has scenes of Vishnu and Śiva, yet more ascetics, but also scenes of men at work and the building of a temple. This western wall to the left illustrates the Churning of the Ocean, but it is so badly worn that little can be distinguished in detail except for the vase of exilir itself and a few effigies of the gods tugging their *nâga* churning-rope. The northern wall shows more palace scenes, a mountain with the usual animals, a sanctuary with closed door near a pool, a procession, and effigies of Śiva, Brahma, Vishnu, Ganeśa and Rahu. The eastern side of this northern wall is devoted to Śiva: Śiva on his bull Nandin, the dual between Śiva and Arjuna, Śiva on his mountain crushing Râvana, Śiva blessing adorers, and more palace scenes and ascetics. The eastern wall (north side) has again a variety of themes: a military parade with musicians, a prince (or king) at the feet of Śiva beside an empty throne, then a pool with two boats and divers at work, next possibly scenes illustrating the legend of how a prince rescued a maiden imprisoned in the rocks, and lastly the story of the Leper King. Here one sees a king in his palace wrestling with a snake which bites him. Servants hasten to consult ascetics in the forest. Women surround the sick king, and then he is seen lying with an ascetic by his side.

114

These scenes provide the only insight into courtly life, religious preoccupations and the life of the ordinary people of Angkor until we come to the account of Chou Ta-kuan, member of a Chinese mission to Angkor at the end of the 13th century (see below). Among such an array of activities depicted on these walls, it is surely significant that not one Buddhist scene appears.

Such knowledge as is now available concerning the history and religious interests of Angkor derives almost entirely from surviving stone inscriptions, which have been discovered and patiently worked on primarily by French scholars over the last 150 years. These inscriptions provide information about the identification of the many temples and definition of their particular territory, with brief life-stories of their founders and their genealogies, either the kings themselves or their high priests and dignitaries, with long lists of the items bequeathed to the temples, presumably so that none should later go astray, and the different classes of slaves attached to them. The long eulogies of the founders and their forebears and the religious sections of the inscriptions are regularly in Sanskrit verse, while the Khmer prose versions relate only to the practical details of the donation, as though not yet equipped with the necessary vocabulary for dynastic bombast and religious concepts. Although both Khmer and Javanese depend upon Sanskrit for the development of a literary language, Khmer seems to have been much slower than Javanese in producing indigenous versions of Sanskrit literary works, let alone an indigenous literature. Thus little or no literature survives from the Angkor period. The development of Khmer literature dates from the later period, probably from the 13th century onwards, when Theravâdin texts in Pâli began to supplant the Sanskrit of the former Brahmanical and Mahâyâna Buddhist traditions.

The absence of any liturgical literature leaves unsolved the question concerning the practice of tantric rites of initiation, such as were common in royal circles in East Java. So far as iconography is concerned, the cult of the great Mahâyâna divinities seems to be limited to the ever popular Avalokiteśvara (Lokeśvara), the "Lady Perfection of Wisdom" (Prajñâpâramitâ), Vajrapâni, who at Phimai seemingly appears in a multi-armed tantric form, with few others scarcely mentioned. Among tantric divinities we seem to know only of Vajrasattva, who represents ritually the self-identification of the tantric yogin in the absolute (*vajra* or adamantine) essence. He is thus identical with Vajrapâni in his supreme rôle as Lord of the *Trilokaçakramandala* (see above). To what extent Khmers were interested in such ritual practices, we can have no knowledge in the absence of the relevant texts.

115

Judging form the several images of Hevajra which have been found, both in Angkor and at unidentified Buddhist sites elsewhere on the Khorat Plateau, of which many examples can be seen in the Bangkok Museum, one is led to assume that the cult of Hevajra was fairly widely practised. But here once again there is no surviving literature to clarify this interesting problem. I note however that these images always show him as a single male divinity, bereft of his feminine partner, Nairâtmyâ, with whom he is always associated

in Tibetan tradition. Perhaps the cult of Hevajra was introduced exceptionally, for whatever reason we cannot know.[77]

It is often assumed nowadays in popular books on Tibetan religion that tantric yoga necessarily involves sexual
yoga, but this is by no means the case. Do we also assume
from this that Khmer practisers of tantric rituals eschewed
all forms of sexual yoga? It would appear so. It seems that
apart from Vajrasattva no other great tantric divinities have
been firmly identified in museum collections. That there
may well have been others is suggested by the discovery of
a rare inscription some 25 kilometres south of Nakhon
Ratchasima in a village named Sab Bâk, dated Śaka 988
(AD 1066), corresponding to the end of the reign of King
Udayâdityavarman (see above). This inscription records
the setting up of a shrine in honour of the Five Buddhas,
seemingly with Vajrasattva supreme as Âdibuddha, at a
place then named Tempâsnaga, by a learned monk Dhanus.
It is especially interesting to note that he followed a reli-
gious tradition of devotion to the tantric cycle known as
Guhyasamâja ("Secret Concourse"), which centres upon
Vajradhara (*alias* Vajrasattva) as supreme Buddha.[78]

116

I have already suggested above, when making deduc-
tions from the little that can be learned from inscriptions
about actual Buddhist practice, that Mahâyânist Buddhist
communities of celibate monks certainly existed, following a regular *Vinaya* (monastic rule), probably that of the
Mûla-sarvâstivâdins. Also certain tantric rituals were involved in their regular practice, specifically those of the
"Four Rites", involving the manipulation of vajra and bell.
From the scarce tantric references available, we may certainly assume that "Adamantine Masters" (*vajrâçârya*) were
available to initiate those with the innate capacities (perhaps also those wealthy enough to pay the necessary fees)
in the realization of enlightenment by the rapid means of
personal self-identification with the master's chosen divinity. In this respect Hevajra appears to have been the
favourite. The general style of Mahâyâna Buddhism in the
Khmer Empire would thus correspond to that existing in
Nepal and Tibet about the same period, but certainly on a

much smaller scale than Tibet, where Buddhism was the official religion of state. Conversely in the Khmer Empire it was a secondary religion, continually relegated in importance to the official Brahmanical cults of Angkor and also in most of the regional capitals. It is impossible to have any clear idea of its impact on the religious life of ordinary people, except to note that they readily welcomed Theravâdin Buddhism, when it later spread into the country (see below).

Popular indigenous literature seems to develop only with the later spread of Theravâdin Buddhism, which had a far more "democratic" appeal. Thus in the early period, so long as the powerful Khmer Empire continued to flourish, nothing exists which is comparable with the wealth of popular literature in Europe from the early Middle Ages onwards. This happily results in our history being very much more than lists of kings and their prelates with reference to their prowess in war together with descriptions of their manifold religious foundations.

117

Adhir Chakravarti has attempted a study of Indo-Khmer civilization, basing his study primarily on the Sdok Kak Thom inscription with its long lists of prestigious brahmanical foundations. The chapters on the workings of the caste-system (pp.87-148) and those on the slave society (pp.149-94) make interesting reading. The general impression gained is that of the extreme laxity of any presumed regulations regarding caste or slave-labour. Notions of caste, relating primarily if not only to those of *brahman* and *kshatriya* rank, were extremely fluid, the one coalescing easily with the other, especially when members of a Brahmanical family married into the family of local rulers, whether in the capital itself or in the provinces. At the same time family-lineage could be of primary significance, but according to circumstances this might be traced through patrilineal or matrilinial connections. If sufficiently self-determined, one could easily concoct false lineages to one's personal advantage. Such was the normal practice of usurpers. At lower levels it is unlikely that anyone suffered the stigma of caste for its own sake, as in India. One notes also that slavery assumed such a variety of forms that it could range from abject servitude to the far better fortunes of a slave-owning "slave".[79]

CHAPTER 6
THE DECLINE OF THE EMPIRE

Jayavarman VII may have reigned until 1219 and was succeeded by his son Indravarman II, to whom his father had
dedicated the main shine at Bantay Chmar. By that time
the decline of the Khmer Empire is marked by the forced
withdrawal from Champa, which henceforth went its own
way, unhindered by attacks from Angkor.[80] The main en-
emies of the Chams however remained the Vietnamese,
who pressed continually south from their earlier home in
the Red River Valley (the area of Tongking now already
absorbed into southern China) until by the 15th century
despite continual resistance Champa was effectively absorbed into Vietnam. At the same time the Thais, previously contemptuously referred to as barbarians and "slaves"
(Syam) in Angkorian inscriptions, were actively establishing themselves in small independent kingdoms in the upper Chao Phraya and Mekhong valleys, gradually displac-
ing or absorbing the earlier Mon population as well as the
more remote Khmer settlements. Thus further south Khmer
regional capitals such as Lopburi were able to detach themselves from the Khmer Empire, becoming effectively independent, until they were in turn overrun by the gradual
Thai advance southwards. It is interesting to note that
Lopburi, claiming independence for a short while, sent
embassies to the Mongol (Chinese) Court between 1289
and 1299.[81] Meanwhile in the course of the 13th century
the two major kingdoms of Chiang Mai and Sukhothai
were founded by successful Thai chieftains, Mangrai and
Rama Khamhaeng, while holding their own against Mongol invasions.[82]

Indravarman II was succeeded by Jayavarman VIII in
1243, who reigned for 52 years. He is generally held responsible for the defacement of the great Buddhist foun-

119

Map 3: Indo-China and the Khmer Empire at its maximum extent
(c. AD 1200)

Map 4: Indo-China today

dations of Jayavarman VII, notably the Bayon and Preah Khan, presumably under the influence of his Brahmanical prelates. The Buddhist images were replaced by Śiva-lingas and Buddhist images in bas-reliefs transformed into Brahmanical ascetics. The main Buddha-image of the Lord seated in meditation under the hood of the Nâga Muçalinda, previously occupying the central shrine of the Bayon, was found during excavations in 1933 broken in pieces and buried 14 metres deep under the central tower. It proved possible to piece it together again, thus reconstituting an image 3.60 metres in height. It has since been enthroned in a small modern shrine erected in an ancient walled enclosure amongst the trees on the right side of the royal route leading from the Phimean-akas to the main eastern gateway of Angkor Thom. I have suggested above that this was probably not the first example of such iconoclastic resentment.

122

Śaivism remained formally the state religion of Angkor under Jayavarman VIII's immediate successors, as is shown by the last Sanskrit inscription, dated 1327, to be set up in Angkor. This was composed by the Brahman scholar Vidhyeśadhîman, who acknowledges himself as servant to three kings, who succeeded Jayavarman VIII, namely Śrîndravarman (1295-1307). Śrîndrajayavarman (1307-27) and Jayavarmâdiparameśvara (1327-?). However, during the reign of Śrîndravarman, who was ruling at the time of Chou Ta-kuan's visit (see below), a Pâli inscription of 1309, the first to be erected at Angkor, records the construction of a vihâra and the consecration of a Buddha-image.[83] As will be shown below, Theravâdin Buddhism was already fast becoming the accepted religion of the majority of Khmer subjects, and there is no indication that this form of Buddhism suffered any persecution. It seems clear that the desecration of Buddha-images was instigated in Brahmanical court circles and was largely limited to royal foundations.

The evidence for this as well other much interesting information derives from the observations noted down by Chou Ta-kuan, who accompanied a Chinese envoy in 1296-97 to Cambodia, presumably sent by the successor of

Kubhai Khan (died 1294) in order to retrieve an embarrassing situation caused by the disappearance of a mission earlier sent to the Khmer court to demand submission. Chou Ta-kuan's descriptions of life in Angkor were included in later more compendious works and have probably suffered considerable abbreviation.[84] There are forty "chapters", the longest about one and a half pages in length and the shortest consisting of only a few lines. The subjects covered include the royal centre of Angkor, houses in general, clothing, functionaries, religious groups, the Cambodian people, childbirth, maidenhood, slaves, language, aborigines (a few lines only), writing (a few lines only), New Year and the season, justice, sickness and leprosy (a few lines only), the dead, agriculture, configuration of the land (very few lines), products, trade (very few lines), Chinese goods (a brief list); the remainder are all very brief except for the last chapter: trees and flowers, birds, animals, vegetables, fish and reptiles, fermented drinks, salt, vinegar and soy, silkworms, utensils, chariots and palanquins, boats, the provinces, the villages, collecting the gall, a prodigy, bathing, immigrants, the army, a public audience given by the king.

123

Even in some of the very brief "chapters" interesting facts emerge. Thus quoting *in toto* the one on villages we read that:

> Each village has its temple or at least a pagoda. No matter how small the village is, it has a local mandarin, called the mai-chieh. Along the highways there are resting places like our post halts; these are called sen-mu (Khmer: samnak). Only recently, during the war with Siam, whole villages have been laid waste.

The statement that Theravâdin Buddhism is represented so widely is interesting. The reference to resting-places along the highways relates to some of the prodigious works of Jayavarman VII already mentioned above. This and the following excerpt may represent the only source for so early an attack by the Thais, which would have had to come through Lopburi and could scarcely have reached anywhere near Angkor.[85] In any case this can only be hearsay. Concerning the Army we read:

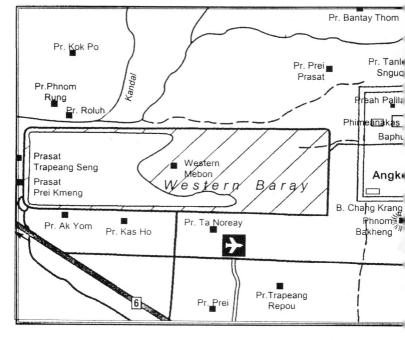

Map 5 The Temples of Angkor

Soldiers also move about unclothed and barefoot. In the right hand is carried a lance, in the left a shield. They have no bows, no arrows, no slings, no missiles, no breastplates, no helmets. I have heard it said that in war with the Siamese, universal military service was required. Generally speaking, these people have neither discipline nor strategy.

It seems doubtful that soldiers went unclothed. On the carvings around the Bayon many of them are wearing short coats.

More substantial is the "chapter on the three religious groups" which covers more than a page:

There are three religious groups, the pan-k'i (= pandits), the chao-ku (= the noble ones) and the pa-ssu-wei (for Skr. tapasvin = ascetics). As for the pandits (the Brahmans) I am unable to say what inherited creed lies behind them, as they have no school of ceremony for training. It is equally difficult to find out what are their sacred books. I have only observed that they dress like men of the people, except that all their lives they wear round their neck a white thread that marks them as men of learning. They often rise to high position. The chao-ku (polite term of address for monks) shave the head, wear yellow robes, bare the right shoulder, knot a strip of yellow cloth around

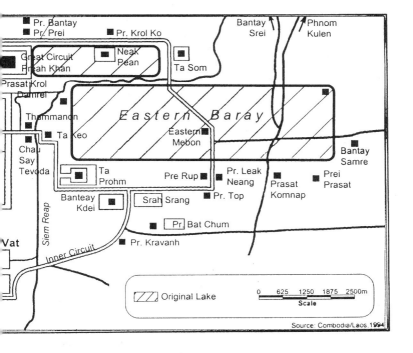

Source: Combodia/Laos.1994

the waist and go barefoot. Their temples, which are often roofed with tiles, contain only one statue in the likeness of Śâkyamuni Buddha, which is called Po-lai (for Khmer: Preah = Lord). Moulded from clay, it is painted in various colours and draped in red. On the other hand the Buddhas on the towers are of bronze. There are no bells, no drums, no cymbals, no banners. The food of the monks is universally fish or meat, which is also set as an offering before the Buddhas, but no wine may be drunk. They content themselves with one meal a day, which is partaken at the house of a patron, no cooking being done in the monasteries. The numerous holy books that they scan are made of strips of palm-leaf, neatly bound together. These strips are covered with black characters, but no brush or ink is used; their manner of writing is a mystery. To certain monks is given the right to use palanquins with golden shafts and parasols with gold or silver handles. These men are consulted by the King on matters of serious import. There are no Buddhist nuns.

The pa-ssu-wei (ascetics, presumably followers of Śiva) are clothed like men of the people, save that on their head they wear a white or red hood. They too have monasteries but smaller than the Buddhist ones, for they do not attain the prosperity of the Buddhist group. They worship nothing but a block of stone (linga).

Lest this text should suggest that these ascetics are well clad, I quote from the chapter on clothing, most of which is otherwise concerned with the royal attire:

Round the waist they wear a small strip of cloth, over which a larger piece is worn when they leave their houses.

Although we have records of the desecration of Buddhist royal foundations, it seems most unlikely that this ever represented a persecution of the religion as such. Thus in the chapter on the "People" we read that : "The worship of the Buddha is universal". Even if this is an exaggeration, it seems clear that by the end of the 13th century Buddhism in its Theravâdin form pervades most of the country, as well as enjoying royal favour. This is confirmed by the "chapter" on the New Year and the seasons, where there is reference to the ceremony of "bringing water to the Buddhas" in which the king takes part. The reference to monks who reach high status at court, being allowed the use of palanquins and parasols, must surely be associated with the accounts we have read above of high Buddhist dignitaries gaining royal favour. It is surely likely that Theravâdin Buddhism only gradually absorbed the earlier monastic establishments of Mahâyâna persuasion and for a while the Buddhist dignitaries at court continued to represent the earlier traditions.

126

Since Chou Ta-kuan expresses ignorance concerning the method of writing in his section on the monks, I quote also the section devoted to "Writing in Cambodia".

For ordinary correspondence, as well as official documents, deerskin or similar parchment is used, which is dyed black. The parchment is cut by the scribe in sizes to suit his needs. A sort of powder resembling Chinese chalk is moulded into small sticks called so (corresponding to a Thai word for "pencil"), which are used to inscribe the parchment with lasting characters.

The chapter on agriculture, with special reference to the rise and fall of the water level in the Great Lake, corresponds closely to the situation with which we are familiar today. As for the products of the country, Chou Ta-kuan lists feathers of the king-fisher, elephant tusks (noting that the best quality is obtained from an elephant hunted and slain for the purpose), rhinoceros horns and beeswax, lacquer-wood, cardamom, gum-resin and "chaulmoogra oil which comes from the seeds of a large tree, the pod resembling that of cocoa but round and containing several score seeds".

Regrettably, the short chapter on trade deals only with small dealings at market level, but we learn from the equally short chapter concerning desirable Chinese goods that the Cambodians were anxious to import Chinese gold and silver, silks, tin-ware, lacquered trays, green porcelain, mercury, vermilion, paper, sulphur, saltpetre, sandalwood, angelica-root, musk, linen and other forms of cloth, umbrellas, iron pots, copper trays, fresh-water pearls, tung oil, bamboo nets, basketry, wooden combs and needles. Chou Ta-Kuan adds: What the Cambodians most urgently need are beans and wheat, but the export of these from China is forbidden.

Chou Ta-kuan is certainly impressed with the city of Angkor. He refers to the city wall with its five gateways, the wide moat which surrounds it and the massive causeways. He notes the gigantic heads of Buddhas which adorn the gateways, and at the centre of the city the Golden Tower (Bayon) and the Tower of Bronze (Baphuon), "a truly astonishing spectacle". He mentions the "eastern lake" which lies four kilometres from the walled city, at the centre of which there stands a stone tower, and in it there lies a recumbent bronze Buddha, from whose navel flows a steady stream of water. Here he may be referring to the famous massive bronze image of Vishnu, which was in fact found in the Western Baray on the site of a ruined temple known as the West Mebon. Dating to the late 11th century, this shrine was built on a small island in the middle of the lake, as was the East Mebon (see page 42), but here the lake is still present, while the Eastern Baray is dry. The Vishnu image can still be seen in the Phnom Penh Museum. "These are the monuments", he exclaims, "which have caused merchants from overseas to speak so often of Cambodia, the rich and the noble".

THE ABANDONMENT OF ANGKOR
AS CAPITAL CITY

Despite its gradual loss of empire, Angkor remained a great and respected city well into the 14th century. In 1352, however, Râmâdhipati, the founder and first king of Ayuthaya, besieged and finally captured it, installing one of his sons on the throne there. It was eventually regained by a Khmer ruler referred to in later chronicles as Râjâdhirâja of the Sun Dynasty, a title rather than a name. From now on the city had to be defended against continual attacks by the Thais, and in 1394, Angkor was again occupied and a Siamese prince installed on the throne, but he was soon assassinated and the Khmers once again regained their capital.

Both Chinese and Cambodian sources confirm the name of the last king who ruled in Angkor as Chao Ponea Yat who took the distinguished name of Sûryavarman on his accession.[86] In the course of his long reign of fifty years, the decision was taken in 1431 to abandon Angkor and transfer the capital to present-day Phnom Penh, at the place known as Çaturmukha (referring to the apparent "four facing" rivers) where the waters of the Tonle Sap merge with those of the Mekhong and the Bassac. Subsequent alternative capitals were Lovek, some 65 kilometres further north, and Oudong, in the same direction but nearer Phnom Penh. It is usually assumed that this decision arose primarily from the difficulty of defending Angkor against continuing Thai assaults, as well as damage done to the whole irrigation system by such constant warfare. These were doubtless important factors, but one has to take into account that the social and economic life of the city had already changed considerably since the days of Jayavarman VII, who could command massive bands of labourers to work on his stupendous monuments. The days of such autocratic kings had passed, simultaneously it might seem with the introduction of Theravâdin Buddhism. While there may be no direct relationship between the two, they were both signs of a great change in the times. Foreign trade was probably now of more importance to the Cambodian economy than reliance upon massive home rice-production, and the move to Phnom Penh suggests immediately removal to a site ideally suited for international trade.[87] Concerning the temporary resuscitation of Angkor in the second half of the 16th century, see below in Chapter 7. From then onwards Cambodia begins to enter the

129

83 *The hill-top site of Oudong, one of the post-Angkor capitals of the Khmer kings, some 60 kms north of Phnom Penh. Owing to the ravaging of the site by the Khmer Rouge, the stûpas have been newly reconstructed.*

modern world, coping as best she could, and often disastrously, with her two neighbours, Thailand and Vietnam, who grow from strength to strength.

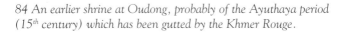

84 *An earlier shrine at Oudong, probably of the Ayuthaya period (15ᵗʰ century) which has been gutted by the Khmer Rouge.*

CHAPTER 7
THE THAI ADVANCE

The fall of Pagan in 1287, resulting from Mongol incursions, left the field open for the Thais, who thus inherited and gradually absorbed all the fruits of these Buddhist labours, which had preceded them, whether literary or architectural.[88] The Thais also had close contact with Nakhon Si Thammarat on the Malay Peninsula, which had gained its independence from Śrîvijaya (see page 8) and which maintained close relations with Ceylon, although not always cordially. Nakhon Si Thammarat had also become an important centre for the promulgation of Theravâdin teachings.[89]

The northern Thai state of Lan Na, with its capital eventually at Chiang Mai, was established in the mid-13th century, while a central state based on the city of Sukhothai, whence they drove the last Khmer garrison about 1220, was well established by the end of the century. Lan Na was built up into a powerful independent Thai state by Mangrai, chief of a small principality at Chiang Saen (now on the far northern Thai border with Laos), by first subduing the neighbouring Thai principalities and then by conquering the ancient Mon kingdom of Haripuñjaya in the upper Mae Ping Valley in 1281. In 1296 Mangrai founded Chiang Mai as his capital, which became a great centre of Theravâdin Buddhism, thanks to the many local monks at his disposal.[90] During the same period, about 1279, Râma Khamhaeng succeeded his brother as king of Sukhothai, then still quite a small state. He seems to have extended it into a small empire, more by persuasion and alliances than by military means, while avoiding conflict with the more powerful neighbouring Thai states such as Lan Na and Phayao to the north and Lopburi to the south.[91] He claims to have ruled with justice over a population that

131

included Mons and Khmers as well as Thais. He is also credited with having invented a script modelled on the Khmer one and adapted to the Thai language, then certainly needed for administration.

While Brahmanical ritual was maintained for court purposes, perhaps following the Khmer practice, Theravâdin Buddhism was richly endowed as the state religion. "Above all else, Sukhothai was a Buddhist state, lavishly supporting a monastic community newly reinforced and invigorated by a celebrated patriarch who had come from Nakhon Si Thammarat. The people of Sukhothai observed the Buddhist precepts and celebrated with exuberance the ceremonies of the religious calendar. The king shared the very throne from which he heard his subjects' plaints and petitions, weekly giving it up that learned monks there might preach the Dharma of the Buddha" (David Wyatt, *Thailand*, pp 54-5). Whoever visits Sukhothai nowadays, maintained as a magnificent archaeological park, gains some moving impressions of the greatness of this particular Thai ruler. Regrettably, on his death the empire of Râma Khamhaeng disintegrated into petty states, maintaining a precarious existence, until in 1438 it was finally incorporated as a province of the rising power of Ayuthaya (named after the famous Indian city of Ayodhya).

132

Mention must also be made of the state of Lan Sang, with its capital at Luang Prabang, which is still on our maps today in a rather reduced form under the name of Laos, with its twin capitals at Luang Prabang and Vientiane. According to a local legend, the founder of this state was an exiled Laotian prince named Fa-ngum, living at the Khmer court. With Khmer assistance he advanced up the Mekong and succeeded in carving out a substantial kingdom for himself in the mid-14th century, extending as far south as the Dangrek Range (the present-day border of Cambodia with Thailand) and bordering on the west with Ayuthaya (Siam) and on the east with Vietnam.[92] Like Cambodia, this state suffered from the pretensions of Ayuthaya and Vietnam, but nevertheless enjoyed relative prosperity and stability up to the 18th century. Its greatest king was Surinyavongsa (c.1637-1694). Thanks to a mission from the Dutch East India Company and the arrival of a party of Jesuits during his reign, there survives European testimony to the generally happy prevailing conditions. The Buddhist religion was well endowed and arts and letters flourished.[93] Soon after his death however disputes over the succession led to a disintegration of the state, resulting in Siamese intervention and eventually to total dependence upon Siam.

Siam now means Ayuthaya, founded as a new city in 1351, thus absorbing the earlier Khmer regional capital of Lopburi with its long Buddhist associations. The assaults of Ayuthaya upon Angkor led to its eventual abandonment, but the contest was maintained by the Khmers throughout the 16th century, based on their new capital at Phnom Penh and the alternative capital of Lovek. They finally lost to the Thais in 1594, and the capital was placed under a Thai military governor. These continual wars caused much destruction around the area of the old capital of Angkor, but inscriptions indicate that King Satha, who ruled from 1576 up the time of his defeat by the Thais

133

85 The Baphuon, like the Bakheng, was turned into a Buddhist sanctuary, probably during the late 16th century, when restoration work was also undertaken at Angkor Vat. The western side of the Baphuon was transformed into an enormous image of Śâkyamuni in the lying posture of his final entry into nirvâna, some 100 metres long.

(or possibly one of his predecessors), reoccupied the city for a while. An inscription of 1577 mentions the repair of "Preah Visnuloka", namely Angkor Vat, while another of 1579 records how he had repaired and re-gilded the great towers of Angkor Vat for the glory of the Buddhist Dharma and consecrated a reliquary to his ancestors and his deceased father. A later inscription of 1587 records the installation of Buddha-images and repairs to "the towers with four faces".[94] Thus Angkor Vat was transformed into a Theravâdin Buddhist shrine, which it has remained until today. The Bakheng and the Baphuon were likewise adapted to Buddhist use, and there are indications that several other smaller shrines were taken over by the

134

86 *A shrine in Bantay Prei Nokor after its adaptation to Buddhism. The* torana *above the lintel illustrates the scenes of the Bodhisattva's flight from the palace on his favourite horse Kanthaka and above the cutting of his hair as a sign of renouncing the world. The Buddha image in the shrine is manifestly new.*

Theravâdins.[95]

A very important ancient royal Khmer site, adapted to Buddhist use, is Phnom Kulen, where Buddhist remains presumably date back at least to the 16th century, if not even earlier. One may note the image of Śâkyamuni laying on his right side as he enters final nirvâna, now enclosed in a modern shrine as a favourite place of pilgrimage on the western side of the southern summit. More unusual are the circles of eight *sîmâ* (boundary stones), indicating a Buddhist ordination site. Two such sets were unearthed. One known as Peam Krei, situated less than two kilometres north of Rong Chen, is decorated with carvings of which ornamental *dharmaçakras* in Dvâravatî style supply the main motif. This can only suggest the arrival of Mon monks in this area, an event that in itself need not be surprising apart from the distance involved.[96]

It should not be thought that the gradual demise of Angkor from the 13th century onwards resulted in total neglect of all creative artistic work. Such traditions continued well into the 16th century, as already indicated by the conversion of many important Angkorian sites to Theravâdin Buddhist usage, as mentioned just above. Thereafter Thai influences prevail, the only architectural creations of note being the Buddhist monastic complexes (Vat), scarcely any now older than the early 20th century, and the royal palace in Phom Penh, all totally in Thai style. The best guide to the whole later period is the important work by Madeleine Giteau, *Iconographie du Cambodge post-Ankorien*, EFEO Paris 1975.

The fall of Ayuthaya to the Burmese in 1767 and the removal of the capital to Bangkok by King Rama I immediately after his accession in 1782 led to a total overhaul of the administration and also of the Buddhist monkhood. However, already by 1785 Thailand was sufficiently reinvigorated to resist a further assault by the Burmese directed at Bangkok. From the end of the century Cambodia fell increasingly under Thai control, becoming effectively a client kingdom, a situation further complicated by the readiness of clients to the Cambodian throne, so often in

135

dispute, to seek the protection and assistance of Vietnam.

This dangerous game of playing one powerful neighbour against another led to the forceful re-entry of the Thais on the scene in the early 18th century. Thus there developed a disastrous situation for the country, aptly described by Professor Hall is his *History of South-East Asia* (pp.459-66) as "The Rape of Cambodia", or in more precise wording: "On either side of the beleaguered kingdom were the two harpies, Vietnam and Siam, snatching away its territories, and each vying with the other in seeking to dominate what was left". Cambodia was only saved from eventual total absorption into the territory of its neighbours (a situation resembling that of Poland from the 18th century onwards) by a treaty made with the French in 1863 and its incorporation in the French colonial empire of Indo-China. Again it is thanks to French insistence that the provinces of Battambang and Siem Reap, including Angkor, were restored to Cambodia in 1907, which has since given French archaeologists and researchers the opportunity of discovering the extraordinary history of the Khmer people, which previously consisted of nothing but legend and fantasy.[97]

NOTE ON THE SPREAD OF THERAVÂDIN BUDDHISM

The spread of Buddhism throughout the maritime states of South-East Asia can be dated from the 5th century AD onwards when Mahâyâna developments are well established in India and certainly prevalent in Ceylon.[98] At this time Theravâdin Buddhism was still only one of alternative forms of early Śrâvaka (Hînayâna) Buddhism. Such Śrâvaka communities existed throughout maritime South-East Asia, as I-tsing readily informs us, but it is evident that the Mahâyâna had greater popular appeal, even if we argue this merely on the basis of the widespread cult of the Bodhisattva Avalokiteśvara. By contrast the major extension of Buddhism across mainland South-East Asia takes place from the 11th century onwards at a time when Theravâdin Buddhism is becoming firmly established in Ceylon under royal decree, and when Buddhism throughout India is on the verge of suffering a devastating reversal. From the 9th to 10th centuries onwards no great missionary endeavours emanate from India except northwards across the Himalayas to Tibet, and even these come to an end by the year 1300. Early forms of Buddhism were implanted in the lower Irrawaddy and Chao Phraya valleys from the 5th century and the evidence suggests that they are mainly but not exclusively Hînayâna. By the time later rulers, such as the Burmese kings of Pagan and soon afterwards the various Thai principalities, begin to deliberately sponsor Buddhism as their state religions, the Theravâdin Buddhism of Ceylon readily presents itself as the one still active and proselytising form of Buddhism.

Only two countries on the Indo-Chinese mainland made any change in their religion, and these are the two that received their religious traditions by the sea-routes of South-East Asia, when Mahâyâna Buddhism was clearly popular and Brahmanical rites were in demand in the royal courts of maritime states. As is well known, these two were the Khmers, where Brahmanical ritual prevailed although Mahâyâna Buddhism held its own, and the Chams on the south-eastern coast who developed a flourishing Hindu-Buddhist civilization, which was finally snuffed out by the Vietnamese in the 17th century. Rather than accept the Chinese religious traditions of the Vietnamese, many Chams opted for Islam, which was then in vogue all along the sea-routes with a small but influential Chinese following.

Conversely, the seeming rapidity with which the Cambodians adopted Theravâdin Buddhism requires some comment. According to the accounts of Chou Ta-kuan, it already had its shrines and temples in every village by the end of the 12th century. This may well be an exaggeration, and some of these temples may still have been Mahâyâna ones in accordance with the earlier traditions. In any case, the change can only have been gradual and it was bound to come about as a result of the momentum given to Theravâdin teachings by the neighbouring Thai principalities, especially Ayuthaya from the time of its foundation in the mid-14th century.

The interesting question arises to what extent Jayavarman VII was personally responsible for the rapidity of the transition.[99] As monarch he was necessarily constrained by court tradition. We must surely assume that his attachment to the Buddhist doctrine was genuine, and architecturally he could only express it in the traditional Mahâyâna form while not totally neglecting the Brahmanical divinities of his court circle. At the same time the numerous "hospitals" and "stage-halts" along his many new highways were dedicated to the Buddha Master of Medicine (*Bhaishajyaguru*). This Buddha-image is usually regarded as a Mahâyâna manifestation, but iconographically it presents nothing, which might be regarded as heterodox by a non-Mahâyânist. He appears as a typical image of the seated Buddha Śâkyamuni, making the gesture of generosity with his right palm turned outwards, while holding his begging bowl with the sole addition of a myrobalan fruit as a typical medical plant. These shrines would have required monks in attendance and Theravâdin monks, assuming some were already available, would have served the purpose quite as readily as Mahâyâna ones. If Jayavarman VII had any serious interest in encouraging Buddhism as the preferred religion of his subjects, in the traditions then prevailing at the time he may have known that the Theravâdin form was the one that held promise for the future. Such a theory helps to explain the rapidity with which it was so widely accepted. There can be no doubt, however, that it became firmly established under Mon and Thai influences, adapting itself largely to these traditions. In race the Khmers and the Thais remain distinct peoples, but in religion they are one and the

138

same, while under the same Mon-Thai influence they are also one with the people of Laos.

At the same time it must be noted that despite the efforts of Rama I to bring some order into the practice of Buddhism following upon the social and religious chaos which engulfed Thailand as the result of the fall of Ayuthaya in 1767, unorthodox forms of Buddhist practice, in dress, in monastic discipline and in various ritual practices continued to have a substantial following. Some of these practices probably had far earlier antecedents, deriving from Mahâyâna and tantric adaptations of the more regular Theravâdin practice, presumably going back to the time when Theravâdin communities were still active in northern India up to about the year 1300. As explained above, there is no separate Mahâyâna Buddhist "sect", as still seems to be commonly believed. Those who gradually accepted Mahâyâna teachings in India from about the lst century AD onwards were all adherents of the earlier Śrâvaka sects, generally remaining faithful to the *Vinaya* (monastic disciple) of their particular sect. It would have been surprising if no Theravâdins had succumbed to this development, which affected so profoundly other early religious sects, notably the Sarvâstivâdins.

When the French began to establish some order in their Indo-Chinese colonial empire, they noted the existence of two Buddhist sects in Cambodia, the *Dhammayutika-nikâya* (literally: "the assembly which holds to the Dharma") and the *Mahâ-nikâya* ("the great assembly"), who were by no means unified in their practices.[100] The first derived directly from the Thai efforts at regulating Buddhist religion, first in their own country and subsequently in Cambodia, a Thai dependency up to the arrival of the French, while the second must have far more complex antecedents by no means exclusive to Cambodia.[101] While Mahâyâna Buddhism in any formal sense had disappeared entirely from Cambodia, a much debilitated form of Brahmanical ritual was still maintained at the royal court.[102]

GLOSSARY

Abhidharma, "Further Dharma", the third part of the Pâli and other early Buddhist canons. It comprises primarily philosophical disquisitions on the nature of phenomenal existence (samsâra) and its relationship to nirvâna.

Apsara (skr.), a celestial maiden.

Bantay (Khmer), a temple-fortress.

Bell (skr. ghantâ) See Vajra below.

Bodhisattva (skr.), a human or supernatural being intent upon the acquisition of enlightenment (*bodhi*). Used in the following contexts:
1. of Śâkyamuni previous to his enlightenment. He is the Bodhisattva *par excellence*.
2. of monks and laymen of the Mahâyâna tradition whose final goal is Buddhahood.

Çittamâtra (skr. "Mind Only" or "Just Thought"), the definitive school of Buddhist philosophy. See below Yogâçâra.

Gandharva (skr.) a celestial musician, several of whom sometimes appear honouring early Buddha-images.

Gopura (skr.) an ornate stone entrance to a palace or temple usually surmounted by a tower.

Hînayâna, the "Inferior Way" of Buddhist practice, according to the followers of the Mahâyana, the "Superior Way".

Homa (skr.), a Brahmanical sacrificial offering, primarily of clarified butter, later adopted in tantric Buddhism.

Jâtaka (skr.), a "birth-story", usually recounting the exploits of the future Buddha Śâkyamuni in his previous lives.

Kâla or Mahâkâla, a fierce protecting divinity. See note 33. His mask appears often on lintels and toranas.

Mandala (skr. mandala) a circle. It may refer to the circle of four continents around the central Mount Meru of Indian tradition, a circle of shrines around a major central shrine, a circle of courtiers around a king or a circle of celestial beings around the main divinity. In symbolic form it often serves as the place of initiation for tantric rituals.

Mandapa (skr. mandapa) the vestibule which opens directly to the main shrine.

Mantra (skr.), a spell, often representing the feminine aspect of a male divinity.

Meru the central mountain of Indian tradition, usually identified with Mount Kailasa.

Mudrâ (skr.), a hand-gesture, as used e.g. to differentiate the images of the Five Buddhas (apart from their different colours). See my *Buddhist Himâlaya*, pp.66-7. For the early use of these hand-gestures. See my *Indo-Tibetan Buddhism*, p.52. In later tantric Buddhism this term can also refer to the feminine partner of a practising tantric yogin. See *Indo-Tibetan Buddhism*, pp.142-3.

Nâga (skr.), a serpent divinity.

Perfection of Wisdom (skr. Prajñâpâramitâ),
(a) the name given to a collection of early sûtras (c. 1st century BC and later) which denounce the theories of the earlier Abhidharma texts.

GLOSSARY

(b) the great goddess of Mahâyâna Buddhism who thus symbolizes this Perfection of Wisdom.

Prâsâda (skr.) a temple. This term is generally used of Khmer temples. Compare Bantay.

Preah (Khmer: *Brah*), a term frequently occurring in the names of Khmer temples. It means "holy" or "sacred", deriving from skr. *vara*. As a noun it means the "Lord" as applied to the Buddha.

Pura (skr. = city, as in many place-names); in Bali: a temple.

Śrâvaka (skr.) lit. "one who listens", usually referring to the early disciples of Śâkyamuni. Thus Śrâvakayâna is a more gracious term for Hînayâna (q.v.).

Stûpa (skr,), in the early period an earthen mound raised over Buddhist sacred relics; later an ornamental shrine, large or small depending upon the circumstances, symbolically patterned according to the relevant period. The supreme example is Borobudur.

Sûtra (skr. literally "thread"), a thread of discourse, a didactic compilation, dealing primarily with Buddhist teachings. Forming the second part of the Buddhist canon, the term may be used of separate works as well as of the whole second part.

Tantra (skr.) a Hindu or Buddhist text of complex ritual, the primary intention being that of self-identification with one's chosen divinity. Buddhist tantras form a separate part of the Tibetan Buddhist Canon, which also comprises Vinaya, Sûtras and the "Perfection of Wisdom" texts, replacing the earlier Abhidharma.

Tantric (an anglicized adjectival form), viz. relating to the tantras.

Torana (skr. torana) an ornamental frontal piece above the lintel, which surmounts the doorway to a shrine.

Valabhi (skr.) seemingly a tower of some kind. See note 50.

Vajra (skr.), Tibetan: Dorje (*rDo-rje*), "thunderbolt", such as the weapon of Jupiter in classical tradition. In Hindu mythology it is the weapon of Indra, god of thunder and war. In Mahâyâna Buddhism it becomes the typical weapon of Vajrapâni, "Vajra-in Hand" and of other Vajra-named divinities. For a good illustration see *Buddhist Himâlaya*, p.38. In tantric rituals it is paired with a Bell, symbolizing Method and Wisdom, the two co-efficients of enlightenment.

Vajrâçârya, earlier a fully qualified master (âçârya) of Buddhist tantric lore, subscribing to the local monastic discipline.

Vat (Thai: Wat), the more recent Khmer term for a monastery (deriving from Pâli).

Vihâra (skr.) a monastery; pronounced in Khmer as "Vihear", as in Preah Vihear (Brah Vihâr).

Vinaya (skr.) monastic discipline, the first part of the Pâli and other early Buddhist canons. .

Yogâçâra ("Yoga-Practice"), a philosophy of the.Mahâyâna, also known as Çittamâtra, attributed to the Bodhisattva Maitreya, who revealed this knowledge to the Sage Asanga (5th century AD). Together with the Madhyamaka it provides the basic philosophy of the later Mahâyâna. See my *Indo-Tibetan Buddhism*, p. 94 ff. It does not represent a separate Buddhist sect, as is sometimes wrongly assumed.

NOTES

[1] The École française de l'Extrême Orient (EFEO) was founded in 1898 and formally established two years later by decree of the President of the French Republic. In function and purpose it corresponds in its initial stage to the Archaeological Survey of India, as instituted at about the same time by the British Government. While the British were concerned with preserving and studying India's vast archaeological past, the French had identical concerns with regard to Indo-China. As its mission the EFEO was responsible for archaeological exploration, for the conservation of monuments, the collecting of manuscripts, and the study of local languages. A major centre was soon established in Hanoi (active until 1959 when the Vietnam War put an end to its activities), and later in 1907 it was given responsibility for the Angkor site, where it remained fully operative until 1975, when the arrival of the Khmer Rouge put a brutal end to all such academic endevours. In 1990 it re-established a centre in Phnom Penh and returned to its former responsibilities for Angkor, but nowadays assisted by various archaeological missions from other countries concerned to assist Cambodia in its recovery. Meanwhile the EFEO has extended its interests throughout much of Asia: Pondicherry in India, in Kyoto (Japan), in Chiang Mai (Thailand), in Kuala Lumpur (Malaysia), while the centre in Hanoi has recently been reopened.

[2] The earliest description of Angkor by a European appears to be that of the Portuguese writer Diogo do Couto (c.1543-1616). See B.P.Grossier, *Angkor et le Cambodge au XVIe siècle*, Paris 1958, p.64 ff. However credit for the effective "rediscovery" of Angkor goes to the French traveller/explorer Henri Mouhot, author of *Travels in the Central Parts of Indo-China*, 2 vols. London 1864. Concerning his life and excepts from his writings, see Victor T. King (editor), *Explorers of South-East Asia, Six Lives*, OUP Kuala Lumpur 1995, pp. 1-50, Chapter 1 by Michael Smithies, "Henry Mouhot 1826-1861".

[3] A succinct account will be found in David P. Chandler, *A History of Cambodia*, Westview Press, Boulder, Colorado USA, also Oxford U.K. 1993, and Silkworms Books, Chiang Mai (Thailand), 1994. More basic material will be found in his *Facing the Cambodian Past*, Silkworms Books, Chiang Mai, 1996. A far more detailed account with numerous personal case-histories is that of Michael Vickery, *Cambodia 1975-1982*, Allen and Unwin, Singapore 1984, 2nd ed. 1985.

[4] Under American pressure the discredited "Democratic Kampuchea" of the Khmer Rouge continued to occupy Cambodia's seat at the UNO. As Vickery aptly observes, "the U.S. treatment of the DK, like its reaction to the Indonesian massacre of 1965 and the policy persued in El Salvador, shows that mass murder is tolerable so long as it is on the right side – the bloodbath is then benign" (*op.cit.*p.290). I would add that the American and Chinese support which was then given to the Khmer Rouge, as consonant with their anti-Vietnamese policies, has surely resulted in the Khmer Rouge still being a power to be reckoned with during the crisis of 1997/98.

[5] One may refer to the important article by Jan Wiseman Christie, "Trade and State Formation in the Malay Peninsula and Sumatra, 300 BC-AD700" in *The Southeast Asian Port and Polity, Rise & Demise*, ed. by J Kathirithamby-Wells and John Villers, Singapore University Press, 1990.

[6] For a succinct archaeological description of Funan, see Bernard P.Groslier, *Indo-chine, carrefour des arts*, Paris 1960, pp. 50-65.

[7] These abbreviated translations are quoted from Paul Wheatley, *The Golden Khersonese*, pp. 48-9. Taking into account a legend that Funan, and later by implication Cambodia, were founded by an Indian brahman, named Kaundinya, armed with a magic bow, which he shot into the boat of a dragon-princess who came out to meet him, thus flightening her into marrying him, the Kaundinya named in the quotation about is sometimes referred to as the second Kaundinya. However they may well be one and the same, as recorded rather differently in a legendary and in a quasi-historical version.

[8] Taken from Paul Wheatley, *The Golden Khersonese*, p.66-7. The original Chinese is from the *Chu-fan-chih* (Description of the Barbarians) by Chao Ju-kua, Commissioner of Foreign Trade in Fukien Province, published in 1226. I note also the article by Michel Jacq-Hergoualc'h, "Temples brahmaniques de l'ancien Tambralinga", especially useful for its up to date bibliography, in *Les apports de l'archéologie à la connaissance des anciens états en Thaïlande*, 3e Symposium franco-thaï, Silpakorn Univerity, Bangkok 1995, pp.218-232. See also the important article by Michel Jacq-Hergoualc'h, Tharapong Srisuchat, Thiva Supajanya and Wichapan Krisanapol, "La région de Nakhon S Thammarat du Ve au XIVe siècle", JA 1996, pp. 361-435

[9] See B.P.Groslier, *op.cit.*, pp.136-7. The important early Cham sites of Mi-son and Dong-duong are now in the Vietnamese province of Quang-nam, respectively 40 and 60 kilometres south of Da-nâng. For fine illustrations of Cham sculpture with a brief historical survey see L. Vandermeersch and J. P. Ducrest, *Le Musée de Sculpture Cam de Da Nang*, as listed in the bibliography.

[10] I draw attention to the impressive work of Robert L. Brown, *The Dvâravatî Wheels of the Law and the Indianization of South-East Asia*, Brill, Leiden 1996, especially useful for its fine plates. The first three chapters provide a very general survey of the relationship between Mon and Khmer states in what are now present-day Thailand and Cambodia.

[11] For the complexities of racial relationships, see H.B.Sarkar, *Cultural Relations between India and South-East Asian Countries*, Delhi 1985, especially Ch.3, "A brief survey of race movements in the linguistic and cultural milieu". Concerning the prehistoric peoples of Malaysia and by implication also Indonesia, see R.O.Winstedt, *A History of Malaya*, Ch.1 "Primitive tribes and prehistorical remains".

[12] See G.Coedès, *The Indianized States of S.E.Asia*, pp.65-6. For his source material see "Le site primitif de Tchen-la", *APKh I*, pp. 53-5. In a much later article, "La stèle de Wat Luong Kau près de Wat P'hu", *APKh I*, pp.367-79, he throws some doubt on this identification owing to the existence of this inscription, which he dates to the second half of the 5th century. It refers to a king named Devânîka, who was crowned here in the name of the divinity of Lingaparvata (= Śiva), whom Coedès identifies as a ruler from Champa. Thus this would then have been a Cham royal site, possibly subsequently captured by the Khmers. It may be significant that Wat Phu remained an important Khmer site well into the 11th and 12th centuries. For a a brief archaeological description of what still remains today, see Michael Freeman, *A Guide to the Khmer temples in Thailand and Laos*, pp. 200-207.

[13] See Coedès, "La Stèle de Ta-Prohm", *APKh II*, pp.11-52.

[14] The legend concerning the Water-nymph or *nâgi* certainly has an Indian origin, transferred to Cambodia. See "La légende de la nâgi",

APKH II, pp.1-3 The quotation concerning human sacrifice derives from Ma-tuan-lin, *Ethnographie des peuples étrangers à la Chine*, translated into French by Marquis d'Hervey de Saint-Denis, Geneva 1883, p. 483.

[15] See David Chandler, *Facing the Cambodian Past*, pp. 119-135.

[16] By means of an ingenious interpretation of the name Georges Coedès (*Indianized States*, pp.36-7) identified T'e-mu, "City of Hunters", with Vyâdhapura, possibly meaning more or less the same, thus urging the Ba Phnom area as the capital of Funan. Later researches now seem to prefer Angkor Borei.

[17] In such a context this suggests that he was qualified in refuting it. Peter Skilling, read a useful paper on "Buddhism in Cambodia in the early period" at the EFEO in Phnom Penh in early February 1997, unfortunately not yet published. He surveys the limited information available for the 6th to 8th centuries from inscriptions and images, relating to the whole area of the extended Khmer empire, as well as Chinese textual references relating to Funan. The inscriptions mainly in Sanskrit and rarely in Khmer relate to grants to unidentified shrines and the erection of Buddha-images, also of Maitreya and Avalokiteśvara, and the occasional naming of monks. One gains the impression that Buddhism, probably mainly in its Mahâyâna form, was well established, but nothing more cogent emerges.

[18] For a general description of this important site see Louis Frédéric, *Sud-Est Asiatique, ses temples, ses sculptures*, Paris 1964, pp. 245-260. For considerable more details see Lunet de Lajonquière, *Inventaire descriptif des monument du Cambodge*, vol. I , Paris 1902, pp.225-236, and H Parmentier, *L'art khmer primitif*, text and plates in two vols., Paris 1927, pp.44-92 and plates i to xxxv.

[19] See Philip Rawson, *The Art of Southeast Asia*, London 1967, pp.13-17; Frits A Wagner, *Indonésie*, Paris 1960, pp.23-7 and Bernet Kempers, *Monumental Bali*, pp.16-31.

[20] See Pisit Charoenwongsa and M.C. Subhadradis Diskul, *Thailand*, Nagel Publishers, Geneva-Paris-Munich, 1978; also C.F.W.Higham, "The Ban Chiang Culture in wider perspective", *Proceedings of the British Academy*, LXIX, 1983, pp.229-261.

[21] Coedès, *Indianized States*, p.37, information deriving from Paul Pelliot, "Le Fou-nan", *BEFEO, III*, p.263 ff.

[22] See I-tsing, *A record of the Buddhist Religion*, p.12. According to a footnote by the translator Takakusu "Poh-nan (Kuo) " is 'Siam' but also includes part of Cambodia". As Siam (Thailand) has no place on the Indo-China mainland in this early period, he can only mean Cambodia. However Poh-nan is clearly an alternative spelling of Funan.

[23] For a brief account see Coedès, *op.cit.* pp 85-6.

[24] See Coedès. *op.cit.* p. 93, deriving from Abû Zaid Hasan, *Voyage du marchand arabe Sulaymân en Inde et en Chine, rédigé en 851, suivi de remarques par Abû Zaid Hasan (vers 916)*, trans & ed. by Gabriel Ferrand, Paris 1922.

[25] Ed. and transl. by G. Coedès and P.Dupont, "Les stèles de Sdok Kak Thom, Phnom Sandak et Prah Vihâr", *APKh II*, pp.167-265. One may note also the discourse of Coedès, "La fondation de la royauté angkorienne et les récentes découvertes archéologiques au Phnom Kulên", *PKh II*, pp.277-285. For a description of this 11th century site of Sdok Kak Thom (which may mean the "Great Reed Lake"), see

Michael Freeman, *Khmer Temples,* pp. 132-5.

[26] Theoretically is could refer to any part of the Malaya peninsula. See Coedès, *APKh* I, p.217 fn.1; he extends the term Java to mean Malay in a generally vague sense, thus including all peoples of the Malay archipelago. Peter Skilling informs me that the Malay spoken by the inhabitants in the southernmost provinces of Thailand is known locally as Javi. It could even refer to Eastern Java, where there was already a Hindu dynasty of Sanjaya's line, antagonistic to Śrívijaya and the Śailendra dynasty of Central Java. Monsieur Olivier de Bernon informs me that Vientiane in Laos was also sometimes referred to as "Java". However none of these seems quite so plausible a reference as Śrívijaya.

[27] This site is a few kilometres from the town of Kampong Cham. A description of the site, referred to as Vat Nokor or Phnom Bachey, can be found in E. Lunet de Lajonquière, *Inventaire descriptif des monuments de Camboge*, vol. I, pp. 92-3.

[28] The most thorough study of the area is that by J. Boulbet and B. Dagens, which was carried out between January 1967 and June 1970, published as "Les sites archéologiques de la région du Bhnam Gûlen (Phnom Kulen)", *Arts Asiatiques XXVII,* special number, Paris 1973. Their work was brought to a sudden end as the result of the revolutionary coup d'état in March 1970, which deposed Sihanouk. Since then until very recently there has been no assured peace in the country and thus this area, like many others, has remained inaccessible. I visited Khnom Kulen in December 1998 and was sad to note the wanton destruction which has overcome this site, as elsewhere in Cambodia. All potentially moveable pieces, unearthed and even cut away from the surrounding rock, have been carried off by the occupying soldiers for eventual sale in the art and antique shops of Bangkok.

145

[29] The upper course of the River, known as Kbâl Spien ("Bridgehead") has happily suffered much less, as many of the stone-carvings are under water and those inscribed on the surrounding rocks are cut in such shallow relief that their removal is impracticable. Boulbet and Dagens refer to an inscription of 1054 recording the decoration of the site with 1000 small lingas by a minister of Sûryavarman I in 1054, while another records the ceremonial visit of Udayâdityavarman II in 1059 and the erection of a golden linga. Phnom Kulen was maintained as a sacred royal city up to the time of Jayavarman VII (1181-1219), and later it was taken over by Theravâdin monks, like other important royal sites.

[30] While accepting this as a possible interpretation, Coedès prefers to understand *Janapada* as a placename. See his short article, "Le site de Janapada d'après une inscription de Prâsâd Khna" in *APKh* I, pp.334-7.

[31] See Boulbet and Dagens, *op.cit.* pp.42-3 and their photos, 121, 122 and 123.

[32] The names of most of these ancient temples are local nick-names, of which the original meaning is now lost. However the name "Sacred Bull" must refer to the three stone imagaes of Nandin, Śiva's mount, which face the three shrines. I draw attention to an interesting article by Elizabeth Moore, "The temple of Preah Ko and the city of Hariharâlaya" in *Studies and reflections of Asian art and archaeology: Essays in honour of HSH Professor Subhadras Diskul,* Bangkok 2538 (Buddhist era = AD 1995).

[33] Kâla or Mahâkâla, the god of time (or eternity), became a popular protective divinity often set up by the entrances to Hindu and Buddhist shrines in India, and his presence seems to be ubiquitous on ancient

toranas in Cambodia. He was equally popular in Central and East Java. Other interpretations have been given, e.g. see Smitthi Siribhadra and others, *Palaces of the Gods, Khmer Art and Architecture in Thailand*, p. 17 f.

[34] The source of the local name of Lolei remains unexplained unless one accepts the suggestion of Coedès that it is an abreviated deformation of Hariharâlaya, once the name of the whole city.

[35] Concerning such religious sects see A.L.Basham, *The Wonder that was India*, p.328 ff.

[36] On this uncertain matter see Coedès, *APKH II*, pp.173-4 (from the article by Coedès and Dupont quoted just above).

[37] See Groslier, *Indo-chine*, p.87: "As the result of circumstances which are ill-defined –prisoner or docile student?– he resides at the court of the Śailendras. He returns to Cambodia towards 790, imbued with Javanese culture and doubtless anxious to imitate it". For a more likely interpretation for "Java", namely Śrîvijaya, see above.

[38] It was closed on my first visit there in July 1997. However since the end of 1998 access has become easy, and in February 1999 I made an enjoyable visit there with Peter Skilling. For a detailed description see Freeman pp.157-73 and *Palaces of the Gods*, pp. 116-33. The authors of this magnificent book are Smitthi Siribhadras and Elizabeth Moore with photography by Michael Freeman. I refer to it hereafter by the short title of *Palaces of the Gods*. Concerning Preah Vihear in particular I draw attention to an invaluable work by John Black, Fellow of the Royal Geographical Society in London, who visited the site from the Thai side in 1955, when the approach-route was by no means so easy as today, and subsequently produced a detailed description, first published in the JSS in two parts, in Vol 44 (1956) and Vol 47 (1959). It was subsequently reprinted as a separate monograph by The Siam Society, Pracandra Printing Press, Bangkok 1976 with the full title of *The Lofty Sanctuary of Khao Phra Vihâr together with the inscriptions, (being) an English translation from learned French sources of all inscriptions associated with the Mountain Temple*.

146

[39] See Frédéric, *Sud-East Asiatique*, p.282, item 304; *Angkor et dix siècles d'art Khmer*, Paris 1977, p.188.

[40] For descriptions of these various sites, see Michael Freeman, *Khmer Temples*, 54-9, pp.64-9, 129-131 and pp.174-5, and *Palaces of the Gods*, pp.78-115.

[41] Being in a remote area under military control, Koh Ker has recently suffered serious depredation, but on this rare occasion the thieves were apprehended. I quote from the weekly *Phnom Penh Post*, 21/3 to 6/3/ 97: "Ten tonnes of stone carvings, hacked off the Koh Ker temple - located in a zone under military control - and cut into pieces were found on an army truck by military police and other authorities on January 30th. The pieces are now at the *Conservation d'Angkor* at Siem Reap." It is indeed deplorable that when works of conservation have now begun again after an interruption of more than 25 years, this work of depredation still continues. Note also the fate of Prâsâd Ta Muen Thom as decribed below.

[42] These are the inscriptions of "Phnom Sandak and Prah Vihâr" (*APKh I*, pp.245-65) included in the article by Coedès & Dupont, relating in the first instant to the inscription of Sdok Kak Thom, q.v.

[43] See *Indianized States*, pp. 116-7; and especially Coedès, "Inscriptions de Bat Chum", *Journal Asiatique* XII (1908), pp.213-254.

[44] Concerning Vat Sithor one may refer to Lunet de Lajonqière, *op.cit.* vol.I, p.167-9, and more substantially to Etienne Aymonier, *Le Camboge*, Paris 1900-4, vol. I, pp.60-70. Apart from the inscription nothing ancient of note seems to remain on this site. For the Sanskrit edition and French translation of this inscription see Coedès, "Un document capital sur le bouddhisme en Indochine, le stèle de Vat Sithor", *Inscriptions du Camboge, VI*, pp. 195-211.

[45] The preferred school of Buddhist philosophy is thus that of "Mind Only" (*Çittamâtra*), representing the latest and "Third Turning" of the Wheel of the Doctrine, as promulgated by the Bodhisattva Maitreya and the Sage Asanga (5th century AD), to whom the basic text of the *Madhyântavibhâga* was believed to have been revealed by Maitreya. See my *Indo-Tibetan Buddhism*, pp. 94-116. This work has been translated with the English title as given above by Theodore Stcherbatsky in *Biblioteca Buddhica*, vol.30, Moscow/Leningrad 1938, reprinted in Calcutta 1971. The *Tattvasamgraha*, as referred to above, is an 8th century work by Śântarakshita, and the commentary was the work of his pupil Kamalaśîla. The text is available in the *Gaekwad Oriental Series, vols XXX and XXXI*, edited by E. Krishnamacharya, with the translation in the same series, *vols. LXXX and LXXXIII*, by Ganthanatha Jha. It may be interesting to note that these favoured Indian scholars played a leading part in the famous debate held in Lhasa towards the end of the 8th century concerning which form of Buddhism was to be followed. See my *Indo-Tibetan Buddhism*, pp. 431-6.

[46] These are the Four Rites of pacifying, prospering, subduing and destroying, commonly referred to and still practised in tantric Buddhism. See my *Indo-Tibetan Buddhism*, p. 238-240; also my *Buddhist Himâlaya*, pp.257-262.

[47] See his *Account of the Buddhist religion as practised in India and the Malay archipelago*, p.10. It is often assumed, quite wrongly, in books on Buddhism, that Buddhists of a Mahâyâna persuasion rejected all the earlier teachings including the ancient rules concerning monastic discipline. Please see my comments on "Continuity in Buddhist Monastic Life" in *Indo-Tibetan Buddhism*, pp.305-15. The *Mûla-sarvâstivâdin* group (where *mûla*, "root" means effectively "fundamental") appear on the scene as a later development from the earlier *Sarvâstivâdin* group, one of the four main groups into which the early divulging Buddhist sects came to be traditionally arranged (see I-tsing, *op. cit.*, pp.xxii-xxiii). They may have developed as a recognized group during the 4th to 5th century AD using pure Sanskrit for the promulgations of their partially revised scriptures. They were thus open to the strong Mahâyana influences which were then in vogue in India, and their *Vinaya* must have presented itself as the most suitable one for use by communities of monks which were then readily adopting as "Buddha-Word" the Mahâyâna treatises of such renowned scholars as Nâgârjuna, Âryadeva, and still later those of Asanga and Vasubandhu of the *Yogâcâra* or *Çittamâra* ("Mind Only") philosophical schools. It came to be widely used in Central Asia and thence in Tibet, as well as throughout South-East Asia until the Theravâdins won over the Indo-Chinese mainland.

[48] Kîrtipandita's inscription contains in Verse 73 a powerful imprecation against iconoclasts: "May those evil men who destroy such merit, experience endlessly the suffering of hell". I note that a similar imprecation is also found in the brief inscription dated AD 982 relating to the Buddhist foundation of Bantay Neang near Montkolborei, some 25 kilometres SE of Sisophon. Concerning the site see L. de Lajonquière, *Inventaire III*, p.424. For the inscription see Coedès, "Stèle

de Phnom Bantây Nâng", *Inscriptions*, vol. II, pp.202-6: "Those who commit continuously the five great sins are less guilty than those who in greed and in violence destroy this foundation of ours. They go to a place of terrible punishments in hell" (extracted from Verses 9-10).

[49] See Coedès, *Indianized States*, p.85 and p.135.

[50] I refer to the article by Coedès and Dupont, "Les stèles de Sdok Kak Thom etc." already quoted above; for this quotation see *APKh II*, pp.233-4. *Valabhi*, which Coedès leaves untranslated here, means in Sanskrit a "pinnacle or raised building or a extra roof-structure". The term appears regularly as one of the items necessary in setting up a temple, usually in association with the required "enclosure". See p.186 and p.227 *op.cit.* for his rather hesitating suggestion of a "building or temple with a flat roof". But why should one always need such an unusual building on a temple site? My own hesitating suggestion at least fits the context.

[51] Concerning these three temples, see Lunet de Lajonquière, *op.cit.* III, pp. 427-444, and Aymonier, *op.cit.* vol II pp.287-302. An English edition is now available of Aymonier's major work in several parts. See *Khmer Heritage in the old Siamese Provinces of Cambodia*, translated by W.E.J.Tips, White Lotus Press, Bangkok 1999, pp.79-96.

[52] For detailed descriptions of these three temples see Michael Freeman, *Khmer Temples*, pp. 214-218.

[53] There were described at the beginning of the 20th century by Etienne Aymonier (see the Bibliography). Vol.II, *Les provinces siamois*, of his massive work has now been translated into English by Walter E.J.Tips, as *Khmer Heritage in Thailand*, White Lotus Press, Bangkok 1999. See especially pages 126-161, beginning with Phnom Wan (Nom Van) onwards.

[54] See Coedès, *Indianized States*, p.136, where he quotes as his source R.C.Majumdar, *Annual Report on Indian Epigraphy* (1949-50), p.4.

[55] Sadâśiva (personal name) is referred to as Jayendravarman in the inscription, the new name bestowed upon him by Udayâdityavarman. As already noted above, a description of the temple, which was built on the route westwards from Angkor towards the latest Khmer acquisitions in the area of the Gulf of Siam, will be found in Freeman, *Khmer Temples*, pp. 132-5. It is in a much ruined condition. See also *Palaces of the Gods*, pp.200-203. I note that these authors use the spelling Sdak Kok Thom.

[56] For a brief description with a selection of photographs of the carvings, see Roveda, Vittorio, *Khmer Mythology*, Bangkok 1997, pp.92-6. It is interesting to note that some of these have only been uncovered recently in the process of the present French programme of reconstruction. They were buried inside an enormous lying Buddha image, part of the later Buddhist readaptations, presumably of the 16th century. See below, pp. 133-5

[57] Pages 144-6. Hall quotes extensively B.P.Groslier, *Angkor et le Camb, age au XVIe siècle d'après les sources portugaises et espagnoles*, Paris 1958, pp.107-21. I note that as part of his argument Groslier quotes appositely Philippe Stern, "Diversité et rhythme de fondations royales khmères", *BEFEO 44* (1954), pp.649-687, where quotations from several inscriptions attest to the primary importance of maintaining these large reservoirs. My brief quotation is from Groslier, pp.116-17. Monsieur Olivier de Bernon has kindly shown me before publication

an article of his entitled "Note sur l'hydraulique théocratique angkorienne", in *BEFEO 84* (1997), pp.340-48. in which he sets down the arguments against this now general assumption, as maintained by Bernard P. Groslier and Jacques Dumar, while reserving a seemingly neutral position himself. The leading opponents of the theory that these great reservoirs were intended for irrigation purposes are W.J.van Liere, Kenneth Hall and Philip Scott, who maintain that there is no evidence of such a use, and that these reservoirs served solely a religious purpose. For the arguments on both sides and the references to the relevant publications, one must refer to the article by Olivier de Bernon just quoted. I note that the latest word on the subject from Jacques Dumarçay is in *Angkor et dix siècles d'art Khmer*, Editions de la Réunion des musées nationaux, 1997, pp.93-100. I would maintain that they were used both for religious and æsthetic purposes by the rulers and the aristocracy and for various practical purposes, including irrigation, by the ordinary people. One may not be quite certain exactly how the water was drawn off for these various purposes, but that it was drawn off would seem reasonably certain. The primary interest of some monarchs, such as in the case of Jayavarman VII and the *Jayatatâka* (see below), may well have been aesthetic/religious, but I doubt if any ruler, however tyrannical, could impose such an enormous task upon subjects who suffered already from excessive impositions with regard the many temples they had to build, unless there were also some benefit for themselves, not to mention the general propriety of the country. The situation probably resembled that of the great early cities of Anuradhapura and Polonnaruwa in Ceylon, where these artifical lakes were popularly known as "tanks" (from Portughese: *tanque*). I quote from R.L.Brohier (previously of the Survey Dept of the Government of Ceylon), *Seeing Ceylon*, Colombo 1965, p.3: "We can but glean shadowy impressions of the vital part these *tanks* played in beautifying the Mahamega or royal pleasure gardens, by filling the bathing pools with water, by providing for the communal needs of the population, and finally by passing the water down to irrigate the rice-fields in the suburbs of the capital." With little change of phrase these words might well apply to Angkor.

[58] By this time the Syam (from which name Siam derives) had already occupied the upper Chao Phraya Valley, and were well known to their Burmese, Khmer and Champa neighbours as auxiliary troops (as in the present case) or as slaves.

[59] For a detailed description of the site see Freeman, *Khmer Temples*, pp. 98-111 and *Palaces of the Gods*, pp.266-305.

[60] Concerning the Mahîdharapura dynasty, see Coedès, *Indianized States*, pp.152-4, and for a description of this whole site, including the local museum, see Michael Freeman, *Khmer Temples*, pp.80-93 and *Palaces of the Gods*, pp.228-65.

[61] The road and the precise number of stages are mentioned in the Preah Khan inscription. See *APKh II*, p.160.

[62] For the inscription see Coedès, "Epigraphie du temple de Phimai", *APKh vol. I*, pp.81-8. Coedès recalls that this Vîrendrâdipativarman is one of the high dignitaries who figures in the grand procession on the carved panels of Angkor Vat and thus is closely associated with Sûryavarman II.

[63] The divinities, of which Vajrapâni's mandala is composed, are listed in the long introduction to the *Sarva-tathâgata-tattva.sangraha, facsimile reproduction* by Lokeśa Chandra and myself, New Delhi 1981, p. 49. I have translated the full account of this triumph over the great Hindu

gods, as recounted in this important tantra, in my *Indo-Tibetan Buddhism*, pp.136-141. I note however that the title Trailokyavijayâ is applied to Prajñâpâramitâ as "Queen of the World" (*Jagadîśvarî*) in the Khmer text of the Bantay Neang inscription. For reference to this inscription see note 48 above.

[64] For a detailed description ssee Freeman, *Khmer temples*, pp.145-50, and for some fine illustrations in *Palace of the Gods*, pp.134-45.

[65] See my *Buddhist Himâlaya*, pp.236-7.

[66] A good description of the carvings with excellent photographs will be found in the recent book of C.M.Bhandari, *Saving Angkor*, Orchid Press, Bangkok 1995; see also Vittorio Roveda, *Khmer Mythology*, pp.100-125.

[67] I note that C.M.Bhandari, *Saving Angkor*, pp.151-3, refutes this theory vigorously. He adduces a rather surprising theory for the anticlockwise direction of the friezes; namely that since the Indian *devanagari* script is written from left to right, so art and sculpture must be likewise "read" left to right. If this were so, all such temples with friezes or a series of paintings would be expected to conform to his rule, and they patently do not. He argues also that no one in the Hindu tradition builds a funeral temple, because the physical remains must be returned to the natural elements. Thus one may well question whether the king's Brahmanical entourage would have agreed to such a procedure. This is a valid point. He suggests also that this great shrine faces west because this is a more convenient approach for a ceremonial procession from Angkor Thom, and in this respect it is fair to point out that other important Khmer temples face directions other than the usual east, simply for reasons of convenience. Preah Vihear faces north while Ta Muen Thom and Phimai face south.

150

[68] This intriguing sandstone monument bears a Khmer inscription, recording the division of authority for a territory known as Jra-reng and subsequent offerings made at the shrine by the ruler of Jra-reng. The dates given for these events are of unclear interpretation. (See Georges Coedès, *Inscriptions de Camboge*, VI, pp.281-2.) Of interest to us is the added proof given of Khmer hegemony in the area probably from the early 11th century onwards.Concerning Prâsâd Narai Jaeng Vaeng, already illustrated, see also Freeman, *Khmer Temples* pp. 192-3.

[69] See Coedès, *The Indianized States*, pp.169-72.

[70] See Michael Freeman, *Khmer Temples*, pp.238-40, noting that he laments the ill-conceived work of restoration, which gives an inadequate idea of the original.

[71] See Coedès, "La stèle de Prah Khan d'Angkor", *Articles sur le pays Khmer*, II, pp.119-166. The verses selected are: 32-36 and 72-77. In this context the "Lotus-Eyed" is presumably Vishnu, although this would be a more suitable epithet for Varuna, god of the Waters. The three,"Watering places" (*tîrtha*) are the three lakes mentioned just above in my text. Concerning "Lokeśa or Lokeśvara and Avalokiteśvara, see note 76.

[72] Having recently measured it, we find it just 6.4 metres square. John Sanday, who first noted this, has also drawn my attention to the traces of the depicting of Buddhist imagery and also traces of colouring on some walls in the inner shrines. See his article on "The Triumphs and Perils of Khmer Architecture" in *Angkor and ten centuries of Khmer art*, National Gallery of Art, Washington, September 1997, pp. 81-92. I

NOTES

note that the French edition, *Angkor et dix siècles d'art Khmer*, Paris 1997, translates the title of this article as "L'architecture Khmer, un colosse aux pieds d'argile".

[73] I note from Maurice Glaize's excellent guide-book, *Les monuments du groupe d'Angkor*, p.141, that the name Palilay derives from "Pârilyyaka", the name of the forest near Kosambhi, where this event is said to have taken place.

[74] See Michael Freeman, *Khmer Temples*, pp. 96-7 and 182-7.

[75] I visited this haunting and suggestive site with Vutthy in January 1999. A succinct description of Bantay Chmar (meaning the "Fortress-temple of Cats", obviously a local nickname) is available in Michael Freeman, op. cit. pp.136-41. Of importance is the article by G.Groslier, "Étude sur le temps passé à la construction d'un grand temple khmer", *BEFEO, XXXV*, pp. 57-68. I note also the article by G.Coedès, "Quelques suggestions sur la méthode à suivre pour interpréter les bas-reliefs de Bantay Chmar et de la galerie extérieur du Bayon", *Articles sur le pays Khmer* I, pp.227-37.

[76] Avalokiteśvara, the Lord who looks down (in compassion) is by far the most popular of bodhisattvas throughout the whole Mahâyâna Buddhist world, while he remains well represented in the earlier period in lands where Theravâdin Buddhism now prevails. (Strangely in China and thus elsewhere in the Far East, where his name was correctly translated as Kuan-Yin, he was popularly treated as "Goddess of Mercy", thus feminine in aspect.) As for his origins, it is probably correct to regard him as representing the future Śâkyamuni, who still as a bodhisattva looked down *(avalokita)* in compassion on the world from the Tuśita Heaven before finally resolving to accept rebirth in order to show the way to salvation to all living beings. At the same time he is often referred to as *Lokeśvara* (Lord of the World), a title which usually applies to Śiva, especially in Khmer texts.

[77] Some good illustrations of these many images of Hevajra can be seen in the catelogue of the exhibion *Angkor et dix siècles d'art khmer*, Editions de la Réunion des musées nationaux, Paris 1997. There is also an article by Wibke Lobo, *L'image de Hevajra et le bouddhisme tantrique*, pp.71-8, but apart from a general description of tantric Buddhism, it adds little precise information concerning the rôle of Hevajra in Cambodia, simply because information is lacking. She suggests that Hevajra may have been referred to as *Vajrin* in Cambodia. However all the contexts in which the name Vajrin appears on inscriptions clearly relates this name to Vajrapâni, just as the abbreviated name Lokeśa refers to Avalokiteśvara. The two abbreviated names often occur together, as may be shown from some of the extracts quoted above. It may seem superfluous to mention in this note my edition of the *Hevajra-Tantra*, London Oriental Series 1959, and several later editions, but I take this opportunity of drawing attention to my later discourses on Hevajra, to be found in my *Indo-Tibetan Buddhism*, especially pp.248-62 and other briefer references to be found in the index.

[78] See the article by Chirapat Prapandvidya, "The Sab Bâk inscription: evidence of an early Vajrayâna Buddhist presence in Thailand", *JSS* 78/2 (1990), pp.10-14. In a very brief bibliography the author refers to other works of Benyotosh Bhattacharya, but fails to mention his edition of the *Guhyasamâja Tantra*, Gaekwad Oriental Series vol. 53, Baroda 1931, or S. Bagchi's later but little improved edition, Darbhanga 1965. There is an English translation based uncritically upon Bagchi's edition by Eiji Takahashi in *Some Studies in Indian History*, Funabashi, Chiba

1981, pp. 135-226. It is regrettable that the Sanskrit edition with the Tibetan version and an English translation, which was ably produced by Francesca Fremantle as a PhD thesis for the University of London in 1971, has still not yet been published. Several of my own translated excerpts will be found in my *Indo-Tibetan Buddhism* by referring to the Index.

[79] See Adhir Chakravarti, *The Sdok Kak Thom inscription: a study in Indo-Khmer civilization*, Calcutta 1978. This work also contains a chapter on kingship and the *devarâja*, which is restated in his *Royal succession in ancient Cambodia*, Asiatic Society Monograph vol. XXVI, Calcutta 1982. Here he estimates the number of matrilineal successions to the throne against the number of patrilineal ones with the suggestion that the earlier represented an pre-Indian practice, while the latter may have resulted from Indian cultural influences. It seems more reasonable to assume that whoever succeeded in achieving the succession, subsequently made use of the most plausible family connections, best of all a direct filial relationship to one's royal parents. No rules could ever have served in this dangerous game.

[80] See Coedès, *Indianized States*, pp.181-2.

[81] *idem* p.208.

[82] Concerning Mongol intrusions into this part of S-E Asia following upon the accession of Kublai Khan as Emperor of China, effectively from 1263 when he founded a new capital at Peking., see primarily Coedès, *Indianized States*, pp. 169-88: "The repercussions of the Mongol Conquests" . One may also see D.K.Wyatt, *Thailand*, see pp. 42-3 with reference to the collapse of the Burmese kingdom of Pagan, and especially pp.48-9 where the Thais themselves were concerned. Fortunately for Cambodia, Champa succeeded in beating off Mongolian attacks, 1281 onwards. See D.G.E.Hall, *History of S.E. Asia*, p.208. Mongol attempts directed at suzerainty over Java were equally unsuccessful; see my *Asian Commitment*, Ch. X under "The Majapahit Dynasty".

[83] Coedès *idem* p.228.

[84] For my quotations from this important document I use the English version, first published by the Siam Society in Bangkok 1987, 3rd ed. 1993, entitled *The Customs of Cambodia* by Chou Ta-kuan, *translated into English from the French version of Paul Pelliot of Chou's Chinese original by J. Gilman d'Arcy Paul*. Pelliot's first French translation was published in the *BEFEO II*, pp.123-77. An amended version was published in Vol.II of his posthumous works, Paris 1915.

[85] By Siam only Sukhothai might be intended, but such an attack seems unlikely. See David Wyatt, *Thailand*, p.58, where he seems to agree.

[86] For a brief account of these last years, see Coedès, *Indianized States*, pp.236-9.

[87] See David P. Chandler, *A History of Cambodia*, pp. 77-8, concerning "The shift from Angkor to Phnom Penh".

[88] The city of Pagan had been built up into a powerful Burmese state by King Anoratha who reigned from 1044 onwards, followed by his successor Kyanzitta (c1086-1112). The Theravâdin canon was collected and re-edited and this form of Buddhism was established as the state religion, close contacts being maintained with Ceylon.

[89] See Coedès, *Indianized States*, pp.184-5. Also Hall, *History*, p.70.

David Wyatt, in *Thailand*, p.51, argues that a Thai ruling family was established there by the mid-13th century.

[90] See Coedès, *ibid.* pp. 208-9, and Wyatt, *ibid.* pp.47-8.

[91] On the cordial relationship between the two neighbouring states of Lan Na and Phayao see Wyatt, *ibid.* p.46. It is interesting to note that its ruler Ngam Müang, who was Mangrai's contemporary, had studied as a youth in Lopburi where he made the acquaintance of another young prince, the future King Râma Khamhaeng.

[92] See David Wyatt, ,Thailand, pp. 83-6 and Hall, S.E.Asia, pp.137-8.

[93] Wyatt, op.cit., pp.120-22. I draw attention to a very recent work, G.F. de Martini, *A New and Interesting Description of the Lao Kingdom*, Bangkok 1998. This work contains extracts concerning Laos from the histories of missions in the Far East by the Jesuit missionary Giovanni Filippo de Marini (1608-82) translated by W.E.J.Tips and Claudio Bertuccio, with a substantial introduction by Luigi Bressan which provides an invaluable survey of other source material. The seeming prosperity of the kingdom is asserted, but the Buddhist religion and the monks in particular are the subject of very harsh criticism, doubtless as a result of the inevitable opposition that the Christian missionaries faced.

[94] See Hall, pp.149-50, and B.P.Groslier, *Angkor et le Camboge au XVIe siècle d'après les sources portugaises et espagnoles,* Paris 1958, pp.17-23.

[95] A large Buddha image was erected on the remodelled summit of the Bakheng, while the upper terrace of the Baphuon was reconstructed in order to make place on the western side for an enormous image of Śâkyamuni lying on his right side in the traditional posture of entering final nirvâna. Here a massive programme of French restoration work is in progress which is unlikely to be completed before the year 2005.

[96] See J.Boulbet and B.Dagens, *op.cit.*, pp.49 ff. noting figures 1-17 and plates 125-34. Once again Peam Krei is a nickname with local unknown associations, seemingly meaning "Harbour of Palanquins". Even the distance may not be so surprising, if one turns to the book by Kamala Tiyavanich, *Forest Recollections, Wandering Monks in Twentieth Century Thailand*, Silkworm Books, Chiang Mai 1997. While her collected material relates primarily to the 20th century, these traditions of monks travelling far afield is very much older.

[97] In this respect I draw attention to the article by Olivier de Bernon, "Le Buddh Damnây, Note sur un texte apocalytique khmer" in *BEFEO 81* (1994), pp. 83-96. This "Prophesy of the Buddha" seems to be a compilation of the 19th century, based upon the supposedly historical prophesy of Śâkyamuni Buddha, as known from early canonical accounts, that his doctrine would endure only 5,000 years. This has been adapted to explain the steady decline of the kingdom from its glorious past under a mythological king Puddum Văns (possibly a vague association with Jayavarman VII who emerged as a known historical figure only in the mid-20th century thanks to French researches, primarily G. Coedès and Philippe Stern), and subsequent catastrophies, beginning with the capture of Lovek by the Thais in 1457. There is no connection whatsoever with Angkor, which was certainly known to exist, but with no memory of its great past.

[98] See the Silkworms Books, Chiang Maiubject by S.Paranvitane, "Mahâyânism in Ceylon" in the *Ceylon Journal of Science*, Section G. - Archaeology, Ethnology, etc. vol.II (Dec. 1928 - Febr. 1933), Colombo, pp. 35-71 with five plates.

[99] It is interesting to note that a son of his named Tâmalinda received ordination as a Theravâdin monk in Ceylon. See Coedès, *Indianized States*, pp.177-8. The source for this is Pe Maung Tin & Luce, *The Glass Palace Chronicle of the Kings of Burma*, a partial translation of the *Hmannan Yazawin*, London 1923, Rangoon reprint 1960, p.142.

[100] The founder of the Dhammayutika-nikâya was Prince Mongkut (1804-1868) of Thailand, who during the reign of his elder half-brother, Rama III, devoted himself entirely to the religious life, gradually creating this reformed religious order (by about the year 1830) in accordance with the customs of Mon monks. On ascending the throne in 1851 he modified some of the changes, primarily those of monastic dress, in accordance with popular demand. See David Wyatt, *Thailand, a short history*, pp.175-91.

[101] The most recent studies carried out on "unorthodox Buddhist practices" in Cambodia are those by François Bizot under the general title of *Recherche sur le bouddhisme khmer*, notably *Le figuier a cinq branches*, EFEO, Paris 1976 and *Le don de soi-même*, EFEO, Paris 1981. Also especially noteworthy is the Doctoral Dissertation of Olivier de Bernon, *Le manuel des maître kammatthân: Étude et présentations de rituels de méditations dans la tradition du bouddhisme khmer*, Paris 2000. I draw attention again to Kamla Tiyavanich, *Forest Recollections, Wandering Monks in 20th-century Thailand*, which provides an important incidental account of the varieties of Buddhist practice encountered by these monks on their wanderings, which certainly included the Khmer districts of Sisophon and Battembang. It also draws attention to the widespread belief in the potentially malevolent operations of local spirits and the need for their propitiation by "spirit-doctors" to the general detriment of the practice of Buddhism.

154

[102] See the article by Olivier de Bernon, "A propos du retour des bakous dans le palais royal de Phnom Penh" in *Etudes Thématiques* 6, *Renouveaux religieux en Asie*, EFEO, Paris 1997, pp 33-58.

BIBLIOGRAPHY

Abbreviations
APKh Articles sur le Pays Khmer, 2 vols, EFEO,
    Paris 1989 and1992
EFEO École française de l'Extrême Orient
BEFEO Bulletin EFEO
CEFEO Cahiers EFEO
East and West, Journal of IsIAO (formerly ISMEO), Rome
IIAS International Institute for Asian Studies, Leiden
JA Journal Asiatique, Paris
JRAS Journal of the Royal Asiatic Society
JSS Journal of the Siam Society

Abû Zaid Hasan, *Voyage du marchand arabe Sulaymân en Inde et en
    Chine, rédigé en 851, suivi de remarques par Abû Zaid Hasan
    (vers 916)*, trans & ed. by Gabriel Ferrand, Paris 1922.
Ang Choulean, see Molyvann.
Angkor et dix siècles d'art Khmer, Réunion des Musées Nationaux,
    Paris 1997, English version: *Angkor and ten centuries of Khmer
    Art*, National Gallery of Art, Washington 1997.
Aymonier, Étienne, *Le Camboge*, 3 vols, Paris 1900-04; An English
    edition is now available of some parts of Aymonier's work.
See *Khmer Heritage the old Siamese Provinces of Cambodia*, and
Khmer Heritage in the old Siamese Provinces of Cambodia,
translated by W.E.J.Tips, White Lotus Press, Bangkok 1999.

Bareau, André, *Les sectes bouddhiques du Petit Véhicule*, Paris 1955
Beal, Samuel, *Si-yu-ki, Buddhist Records of the Western World*,
    London 1884, reprinted in Delhi 1969.
de Bernon, Olivier, "Le Buddh Damnây, note sur un texte
    apocalytique khmer", BEFEO 81 (1994), pp.83-96;
 - *idem* "Note sur l'hydraulique théocratique angkorienne", BEFEO
84 (1997), pp.340-48;
 - *idem* "A propos du retour des bakous dans le palais royal de
    Phnom Penh" in *Études thématiques 6, Renouveaux religieux en
    Asia*, EFEO Paris 1997, pp.33-58.
Bhandari, C.M. *Saving Angkor*, Orchid Press, Bangkok 1995.
Bizot, François, *Le don de soi-même*, EFEO, Paris 1981;
 - *idem Le figuier a cinq branches*, EFEO, Paris 1976;
 - *idem Râmakem ou l'amour symbolique de Râma et Seta*, EFEO, Paris
1989.
Black, John, *The Lofty Sanctuary of Khao Phra Vihâr*, the Siam
    Society, Bangkok 1976.
Briggs, L.P., *The Ancient Khmer Empire*, Transactions of the
    American Philosophical Society, new series, Vol.41,
    Philadelphia 1951, reprinted 1962, 1964. Recently reprinted in a
    new edition by White Lotus Press, Bangkok 1999.
Brown, Robert L. *The Dvâravatî Wheels of the Law and the
    Indianization of South East Asia*, Brill, Leiden 1996.
Boulbet, J and Dagens B. "Les sites archéologiques de la région du
    Bhnam Gûlem (Phnom Kulen)", *Arts Asiatiques XXVII*, special
    number, Paris 1973. Bandung, 1956;

Chakravati, Adhir, *Royal Succession in Ancient Cambodia*, Asiatic Society Monograph xxvi, Calcutta 1982;
- *idem The Sdok Kak Thom Inscription: a study in Indo-Khmer civilization*, Calcutta 1978.
Chandler, David P. *A History of Cambodia*, Westview Press, Boulder, Colorado USA, also Oxford UK 1993, and Silkworms Books, Chiang Mai (Thailand) 1994;
- *idem Facing the Cambodian Past*, Silkworms Books, 1996;
- *idem* see Mabbett.
Coedès, G. *The Indianized States of South-East Asia* in the English edition as published by the East-West Center Press, 1968 (since 1971, known as the University Press of Hawai). From the original French: *Les états hindouisés d'Indochine et d'Indonésie*, Paris 1948, reprinted by Editions E. de Boccard, Paris 1964;
- *idem Articles sur le pays Khmer*, EFEO, Paris, 2 vols, 1989 and 1992;
- *idem* "Les capitales de Jayavarman II, *BEFEO XXVIII* , p.117 ff. (*APKh I*, pp.127-37);
- *idem* "Un document capital sur le bouddhisme en Indochine, la stèle de Vat Sithor", *Inscriptions du Camboge*, VI, pp.195-211;
- *idem* " Epigraphie du temple de Phimai", *BEFEO XXIV*, p.345 ff. (*APKh I*, pp.81-8);
- *idem* "La fondation de la royauté angkorienne et les récentes découvertes archéo- logiques au Phnom Kulên", *CEFEO 14*, 1938, pp.40-48 (*APKh II*, pp.277-85);
- *idem* "La légende der la nâgi", *BEFEO XI*, p.391 ff. (*APKh II*, pp.1-3);
- *idem* "Inscriptions de Bat Chum", *JA XII* (1908), pp.213-54;
- *idem* "Quelques suggestions sur la méthode à suivre pour interpréter les bas-reliefs de Bantay Chmar et de la galerie extérieur du Bayon", *BEFEO XXXII*, p.71 ff. (*APKh, II*, pp.229 39);
- *idem* "Le site de Janapada d'après une inscription de Prasad Khna", *BEFEO XLIII*, pp.1-16 (*APKh I*, pp.334-7);
- *idem* "Le site primitif de Tchen-la", *BEFEO XVIII*,9,p.1 ff. (*APKh I*, pp.53-5);
- *idem* "La stèle de Prah Khan d'Angkor", *BEFEO XLI*, pp.255-301 (*APKh II*, pp.119-66);
- *idem* "La stèle di Phnom Bantây Nâng". *Inscriptions du Camboge II*, pp.202-206;
- *idem* "La stèle de Ta-Prohm", *BEFEO VI*, pp.44-85 (*APKh II*, pp.11-52);
- *idem* "La stèle de Wat Luong Kau près de Wat P'hu", *BEFEO XLVIII*, pp.209-20 (*APKh I*, pp.367-79).
Coedès G. & Dupont, P. "Les stèles de Sdok Kak Thom, Phnom Sandak et Prah Vihâr", *BEFEO XLIII*, p.56 ff. (*APKh II*, pp.167-265).

Dagens, B. see Boulbet.
De Martini, G.F. *A New and Interesting Description of the Lao Kingdom*, based on *Delle missioni dei padri della compagnia di Gesu nella Provincia del Giappone*, 1663, N.A.Tinassi, Rome and on an extract published as *Relation nouvelle et curieuse du Royaume de Lao*, 1966, Gervais Couzier, Paris, translated by Walter Tips and Claudio Bertuccio, introduction by Luigi Bressan, Bangkok 1998.

Ferrand, Gabriel, see Abû Zaid Hasan.

Fonteyn, Jan, *The Sculpture of Indonesia*, National Gallery of Art, Washington DC 1990.

Frédéric, Louis, *Sud-East Asiatique, ses temples, ses sculptures*, Paris 1964.
- *idem* see Nou.

Freeman, Michael, *A Guide to Khmer Temples in Thailand and Laos*, River Books, Bangkok 1996;
- *idem* see Moore, Elizabeth;
- *idem* see Smitthi Siribhadra.

Giteau, Madeleine, *Iconographie du Cambodge post-Angkorienne*, EFEO Paris 1975
- idem "Note sur Kumbhakarna dans l'iconographie khmer", *Arts Asiatiques* (1995), pp. 69-75.

Glaize, Maurice, *Les monuments du groupe d'Angkor*, Adrien Maisonneuve, Paris 1963, new edition 1993, entitled simply *Angkor*.

Groslier, Bernand P. *Angkor et le Camboge au XVIe siècle d'après les sources portugaises et espagnoles*, Paris 1958;
- idem *Indo-chine, carrefour des arts*, Paris 1960;
- idem "Étude sur le temps passé à la construction d'un grand temple Khmer", *BEFEO XXXV*, pp. 57-68.

Hall, D.G.E. *A History of South-East Asia*, Macmillan Press, London 1955 and numerous reprints, of which the 1994 edition is to hand.

Higham, C.F.W., "The Ban Chiang Culture in wider perspective", *Proceedings of the British Academy*, *LXIX* (1983), pp.229-261.

Hirth, Friedrich and Rockhill, W.W. *Chau Ju-kua, his work on the Chinese and Arab trade in the twelfth and thirteen centuries*, St Petersburg 1911.

I-tsing, *A record of the Buddhist religion as practised in India and the Malay Peninsula, AD 671-695*, translated by Takakusu, Oxford 1868.

Iyer, Alessandra, *Prambanan: Sculpture and Dance in Ancient Java*, Bangkok 1997.

Jacob, Judith, *The traditional literature of Cambodia*, OUP London 1996;
- *idem* and Kuoch Haksrea, trans. *Reamker, The Cambodian Version of the Ramayana*, RAS London 1986.

Jacq-Hergoualc'h, Michel, "Une cité-état de la Péninsule Malaise: le Lankasuka", *Arts Asiatiques L* (1995), pp. 47-64;
- *idem* "Un example de civilization de ports-entrepôts des Mers du Sud: le Sud Kedah (Malaysia) Ve - XIVe siècles", *Arts Asiatiques XLVII (1992), pp. 40-48*;
- *idem* "Temples brahmaniques de l'ancien Tambralinga" in *Les apports de l'archéologie à la connaissance des anciens états en Thailande*, Silpakom University, Bangkok 1995;
- *idem* in cooperation with Tharapong Srisuchat, Thiva Supajanya and Wichapan Krisanapol, "La région de Nakhon Si Thammarat du Ve au XIVe siècle", *JA 1996*, pp.361-435.

- *idem* "Archaeological Research in the Malay Peninsular", JSS 85 (1997), 121-32;
- *idem* with T. Supajanya & W. Krisanapol, "Une étape maritime de la route de la soie: la partie méridionale de l´isthmus de Krau au IXe siècle", JA. 1998, pp. 235-320.

Krom, N.J. *Barabudur:Archaeological Description*, the Hague 1927, 2 vols of text and 2 vols of plates; reprinted by the Rin-chen Book Company, Japan, 1993, 2 vols of text, one volume comprising Krom's 2 vols of plates, and an additional volume of T. van Erp's *Architectural Description*.

Lunet de Lajonquière, É. *Inventaire descriptif des monuments du Camboge*, 3 vols, Paris 1902-11.

Mabbett, Ian and David Chandler, *The Khmers*, Blackwell, Oxford 1995.

Molyvann, Vann (editor), Ang Choulean, Eric Prenowitz & Ashley Thompson, *Angkor, a manual for the Past. Present and Future*, Apsara, publication of the Cambodian Government 1996. A French version was published in 1997.

Moore.E, "The temple of Preah Ko and the city of Hariharâlaya" in *Studies and reflections of Asian art and archaeology: Essays in honour of HSH Professor Subhadras Diskul*, Bangkok 2538 (=AD 1995).

Moore, Elizabeth with Philip Stott, Sriyavudh Sukhasvasti & Michael Freeman, *Ancient Capitals of Thailand*, Asia Books, Bangkok 1996;

Moore, Elizabeth and Anthony Freeman, "Circular sites at Angkor: a radar scattering model", JSS 85 (1997), pp.107-119;
- *idem* see Smitthi Siribhadra;

Ma-tuan-lin, *Ethnographie des peuples étrangers à la Chine*, French translation by Marquis d'Hervey de Saint-Denis, Geneva 1883.

Niharranjan Ray, *Sanskrit Buddhism in Burma*, Calcutta 1936, Orchid Press, Bangkok 2001

Nou, Jean-Louis and Frédéric, Louis, *Borobudur*, Paris and Rome, 1994.

Paranvitane, S. "Mahâyânism in Ceylon", *Ceylon Journal of Science, Section G.-Archaeologiy, Ethnologie, etc. vol.II* (Dec.1928-Febr.1933), Colombo, pp.35-71.

Parmentier, H. *L'art Khmer primitif*, 2 vols of text and plates, Paris 1927.
- *idem* "Complément à l'art Khmer primitif", *BEFEO XXXV* (1935).

Pelliot, Paul, "Le Fou-nan", *BEFEO III*, *p.263 ff*.

Pisit Charoenwongs and Subhadradis Diskul, *Thailand*, Nagel Publishers, Geneva/Paris/Munich 1978 (in the *Archaeologia Mundi* series of Jean .

Prenowitz, Eric, see Molyvann.

Rawson, Philip, *The Art of Southeast Asia*, London 1967 and later editions.

Richardson H.E. *Adventures of a Tibetan fighting monk*, Tamarind Press, Bangkok, 1986;

- idem (in collaboration with David Snellgrove q.v.) *A Cultural History of Tibet;*
- idem *A Corpus of Tibetan Inscriptions*, RAS, London 1985;
- idem *High Peaks, Pure Earth, Collected Writings on Tibetan History and Culture*, Serindia, London 1998;
- idem *Tibet and its History*, O.U.P. London 1962.

Sakar, H.B. *Cultural Relations between India and Southeast Asian Countries*, Delhi 1985.

Skilling, Peter, "The advent of Theravâdin Buddhism to mainland South-East Asia", *JIABS* 20.1 (1997), pp.93-107,
- idem "Buddhism in Cambodia in the Early Period", Paper read to the EFEO in Phnom Penh, early February 1997;
- idem "A citation from the *Buddhavamsa* of the Abhayagiri school", *JPTS* XVIII (1933), pp.165-75,
- idem "Dharmakîrti's Durbodhâloka and the literature of Śrîvijaya", *JSS* 85 (1997), pp.187-194.

Smitthi Siribhadra, Elizabeth Moore, Michael Freeman, *Palaces of the Gods, Khmer Art & Architecture in Thailand*, River Books, London 1992.

Snellgrove, D.L., *Asian Commitment*, Travels and Studies in the Indian Sub-Continent and South-East Asia, Orchid Press, Bangkok 2000
- idem "Borobudur: Stûpa or Mandala", *East and West 46* (1996), pp.477-483;
- idem *Buddhist Himâlaya*, Cassier, Oxford 1957, reprinted by Himalayan Bookseller, Kathmandu, 1995;
- idem *The Hevajra Tantra*, 2 vols, OUP, London, 1959 and later reprints, now forthcoming Orchid Press, Bangkok;
- idem *Indo-Tibetan Buddhism*, Serindia Publications, London 1987, now forthcoming Orchid Press, Bangkok;
- idem *Himalayan Pilgrimage*, Cassier, Oxford, 1961; first American edition by Prajña Press, Great Eastern Book Company, Boulder, 1981; later editions by Shambhala Publications, Boston, now forthcoming Orchid Press, Bangkok.

Snellgrove, D.L. (general editor), *The Image of the Buddha*, UNESCO 1978.

Snellgrove D.L. & Richardson Hugh, *A Cultural History of Tibet*, London 1968 and later reprints by Shambhala, Boston, 1968 and 1995.

Snellgrove, D.L. and Tadeusz Skorupski, *The Cultural Heritage of Ladakh*, 2 vols, Warminster 1979 and 1980.

Stott, Philip see Moore Elizabeth.

Stuart-Fox, M. and Bunhaeng Ung, *The Murderous Revolution*, Orchid Press, Bangkok 1986.

Subhadradis Diskul, M.C. (editor and contributor) *The Art of Srîvijaya*, UNESCO, 1980;
- idem see Pisit Charoenwongsa.

Thompson, Ashley, see Molyvann.

Tipps, W.E.J. see Aymonier and Di Martini.

Tiyavanich, Kamala, *Forest Recollections, Wandering Monks in 20th century Thailand*, Silkworm Books, Chiang Mai, 1997.

Vandermeersch, Léon & Ducrest, Jean Pierre, *Le Musée de Sculpture*

Cam de Da Nâng, Éditions de l'Association francaise des Amis de
l'Orient, Paris 1997.

Vickery, Michael T, *Cambodia 1975-1982*, Allen and Unwin,
Singapore 1984, 1985;
- idem *Cambodia after Angkor*, a disertation presented to Yale
University as a Ph.D. Thesis, 2 vols, December 1977,
- idem *Society, Economics and Politics in Pre-Angkor –Cambodia*,
Tokyo 1998.

Wagner, Fritz, *Indonésie, art d'un archipel*, ed. Albin Michel, Paris
1960.

Wheatley, Paul, *The Golden Khersonese, Studies in the historical
geography of the Malay Peninsular before 1500*, Kuala Lumpur 1961;
- idem *Impressions of the Malay Peninsular in Ancient Times*, Singapore
1964.

Winstedt, R.O. *A History of Malaya*, Singapore edition 1962.

Wiseman Christie, Jan, "Trade and State formation in the Malay
Peninsular and Sumatra" in *The Southeast Asian Port and Polity,
Rise and demise*, ed. Kathirithamby-Wells J. and John Villiers,
Singapore University Press, 1990.

Wyatt, David, *Thailand*, Yale University Press, Newhaven 1982.

Index

161

162

163

The continuing wanton destruction fo Khmer temples by thieving professionals : a notorious example.

A 6-metre-long section of the surrounding wall (over 2 metres high) at Bantay Chmar with surface carvings of series of lifesize images of the Great Bodhisattva Avalokiteśvara was recently systematically dismantled by thieves for eventual sale to art-dealers. Fortunately on this rare occasion the trucks containing the numbered pieces were apprehended by the Thai police and this important work of art has since been returned to Cambodia. This photograph shows the surviving end of the broken wall at Bantay Chmar. See also pp. 105-8.